1825

THINK. BUILD. THRIVE.

Balaji Sunku

notionpress.com

INDIA • SINGAPORE • MALAYSIA

ISBN
Paperback 9798899294976
Hardcase 9798899294983

Contents

Part IV: Becoming Your Best Self

Part V: The Big Picture

Acknowledgement

No journey is ever taken alone, and this book is no exception. I am deeply grateful to the people who have stood by me, shaped me, and guided me through my life's most challenging and transformative moments.

First and foremost, to my father, your unwavering belief in me has been my anchor during the storms. When I fell hard, you were there to lift me, guiding my career like a compass and helping me find direction when everything felt uncertain. Your wisdom and steady presence have been invaluable, and I wouldn't be here without your guidance.

To my mother, your love is a healing force that has carried me through my toughest days. Your ability to lift me, even in the darkest moments, and your unwavering support in everything I pursue mean more to me than words can express. From helping me with my work to offering real-life advice, your presence has been a source of strength and clarity in every chapter of my life.

To my younger sister, you've been both a supporter and a teacher. I've learned so much from you; your quiet strength and constant encouragement have been essential to everything I've achieved. Without your support, much of what I've done would not have been possible. Your belief in me is a gift I cherish deeply.

To my grandparents, uncle, aunt, and my friends who supported me in writing this book. Your support gave me strength during this journey, and for that, I am truly grateful.

Each of you has touched my life in ways that extend far beyond these pages. This book is not just a reflection of my work; it is a testament to the love, guidance, and support you've given me. From the bottom of my heart, thank you for being a part of this journey.

Preface

The years between 18 and 25 are exhilarating, confusing, and transformative. It's a time when ambition burns bright, and the world seems filled with endless possibilities. Yet, it's also a phase where uncertainty looms; everyone expects you to figure life out, but no one hands you a clear guide. This book is the one I wish I had during those years as a roadmap to navigate the most defining stage of your life with purpose, clarity, and confidence.

Why does this stage matter so much? Because the choices you make now shape everything that comes after. These years are when you begin to dream bigger, face reality, and build the foundation for the future you want. Whether you're stepping into adulthood, discovering who you are, or chasing your wildest ambitions, this is your time. And how you use these years will determine the kind of life you lead.

But let me be real with you: It's not always easy. I've been there. I know what it feels like to be hungry for more yet overwhelmed by the weight of uncertainty. There were nights I lay awake wondering if I was on the right path. There were days when I questioned my potential, when the fear of failure was louder than my dreams. And if you've ever felt like that, trust me, you're not alone.

From my own experience and guidance, I wrote this book, 1825: Think. Build. Thrive. This book isn't just a collection of ideas; it's a framework to help you take action. It's the guide I wish someone had handed me while trying to figure it all out. Within these pages, you'll find real stories from people who turned ambition into reality, science-backed strategies that reveal how to thrive, and practical exercises to help you apply every lesson to your own life.

This book is for the dreamers who refuse to settle. It's for those who feel the fire to achieve more, but also know how easy it is to get lost along the way. Whether you want to master self-discipline, break through procrastination, or balance ambition with patience, this book will equip you with the tools to think big, build your path, and thrive in every area of life.

But beyond the strategies and frameworks, there's something deeper I want you to take away. You have the power to shape your future. No matter where you come from, no matter how uncertain things feel right now, you are capable of creating a life that reflects your boldest dreams. Every small decision you make today and every effort you invest become a brick in the foundation of your future.

I didn't write this book to tell you what to do. I wrote it to empower you to take charge of your own journey. Because the truth is, no one else is going to do it for you. And while the path isn't always clear, I can promise you this: you are capable of more than you realise. Your dreams are valid. Your ambitions are worth pursuing. And your future is yours to shape.

So as you turn these pages, I want you to ask yourself some big questions:

1. What kind of life do I want to create?
2. Who do I want to become?
3. What kind of legacy do I want to leave behind?

These questions aren't easy, but answering them will change everything. And no matter where you are today, it's never too early or too late to start.

This book is your guide, but the journey is yours. Are you ready to think big, build your path, and thrive? Because the future is waiting and starts right here, right now.

Introduction: Why This Book Matters

The Journey Between 18 and 25

There's something uniquely magical—and terrifying—about the years between 18 and 25. For most of us, this is the time when we experience the most profound personal growth, yet it can feel like we're stumbling through it without a map. It's a paradox: the world tells us these are our "freedom years", yet they're also the years when we're expected to figure out what to do with the rest of our lives.

Whether you're pursuing higher education, starting your career, exploring your passions, or navigating relationships, one thing is certain: **the choices you make today will echo throughout your future**. These are the years when you build the foundation for the person you'll become.

But here's the secret: you don't have to do it perfectly. The goal isn't to create a flawless life plan; it's to learn how to adapt, grow, and make progress—even when things don't go according to plan.

Why Focus on 1825?

The name of this book is deliberate. Ages 18 to 25 are often referred to as the "defining decade", a time when the brain is still developing and habits are easier to form. Researchers have found that by age 25, the brain's prefrontal cortex, responsible for decision-making and impulse control, has largely finished maturing. This means that the way you handle choices, challenges, and setbacks during this time will shape your behaviour for years to come.

These years are also unique because:

1. **You're in a season of possibility.** You're old enough to make your own decisions but young enough to experiment and recover from mistakes.
2. **You have the freedom to explore.** Whether it's your career, identity, or relationships, this is the time to try new things and discover what truly matters to you.
3. **You're laying the groundwork for the future.** While it's tempting to think of "later" as the time to get serious about life, the truth is that the earlier you start, the more options you'll have down the road.

What This Book Offers

Let's be clear—this isn't a book filled with vague motivational quotes or one-size-fits-all advice. It's a **framework** for success tailored to the challenges and opportunities of the 18–25 age group. It's practical, actionable, and grounded in real-world examples.

By the time you finish this book, you'll:

1. Understand how to set and achieve meaningful goals.

2. Learn to navigate challenges like failure, stress, and self-doubt.
3. Build habits that will serve you well into adulthood.
4. Balance ambition with self-care and relationships.
5. Gain confidence in your ability to shape your future.

A Glimpse Into the Framework

This book is built around five pillars:

1. **Clarity**: Knowing what you want is the foundation of all success. This book will help you define your vision and align your actions with your goals.
2. **Discipline**: Success doesn't happen overnight. You'll learn how to build small, consistent habits that lead to big results.
3. **Resilience**: Failure isn't the end; it's part of the process. This book will teach you how to bounce back stronger.
4. **Balance**: Life isn't just about work. You'll explore how to cultivate meaningful relationships, take care of your health, and still chase your dreams.
5. **Growth Mindset**: Instead of fearing challenges, you'll learn to embrace them as opportunities to learn and grow.

Who This Book Is For

This book is for the dreamers and the doers. It's for the students, the entrepreneurs, the artists, the professionals, and everyone in between. It's for anyone who has ever asked themselves:

1. "What should I do with my life?"
2. "How do I balance everything?"
3. "Am I doing enough?"

Whether you're full of ambition or struggling to figure out your next step, this book is here to help.

An Inspiring Story

Imagine being 30 years old, ousted from the company you helped build, and feeling like a failure. That was the reality for Steve Jobs in 1985. But instead of giving up, he used that setback as a springboard to reflect, innovate, and grow. He went on to create NeXT and revitalize Pixar. When he returned to Apple in 1997, he transformed it into one of the most successful companies in the world.

Stories like this remind us that success isn't a straight line. It's a journey filled with twists, turns, and moments of doubt. What matters is how you respond to the challenges and opportunities along the way.

How to Read This Book

Think of this book as your personal guide.

1. **Take it step by step.** Each chapter builds on the one before it, so there's no need to rush.
2. **Do the exercises.** This book isn't just about reading; it's about taking action. Reflect on the questions, complete the tasks, and watch your progress unfold.

3. **Revisit as needed.** The lessons in this book are timeless, so don't hesitate to return to them whenever you need a refresher.

Closing Thoughts

This is your time. The choices you make, the habits you build, and the mindset you cultivate during these years will shape your life in ways you can't yet imagine. The journey won't always be easy, but it will be worth it. By the end of this book, you'll have the tools, confidence, and clarity to make the most of these defining years. So let's get started— you've got a bright future ahead.

Part I

The Foundation

CHAPTER 1

Why 1825?

The Transformative Years That Define Your Life

Introduction: The Power of a Decade

When you think about ages 18 to 25, what comes to mind? For some, it's the excitement of newfound independence—moving out, pursuing a degree, or landing that first job. For others, it's uncertainty: "What should I do? Am I on the right track?"

Here's the truth: These seven years are a gift. They're a time of immense potential, where every decision you make carries more weight than you might realise. Whether you're forging a career, discovering your passions, or building relationships, these are the years where the foundation of your future is laid.

"Don't let the fear of making the wrong decision paralyse you. What matters most is that you're building momentum."

1. The Science of Growth Between 18 and 25

Your Brain's Final Frontier

The human brain continues to develop until around the age of 25, particularly in the **prefrontal cortex**, the region responsible for decision-making, impulse control, and planning.

1. What This Means:

During these years, you're biologically primed to:

1. Learn new skills quickly.
2. Adapt to changing environments.
3. Form habits that last a lifetime.

2. Neuroplasticity:

The brain's ability to rewire itself is especially strong in young adulthood. This is why learning a language, starting a business, or mastering a craft feels easier now than it might later.

"Your brain is your greatest ally. Feed it new challenges and experiences while it's at its peak of adaptability."

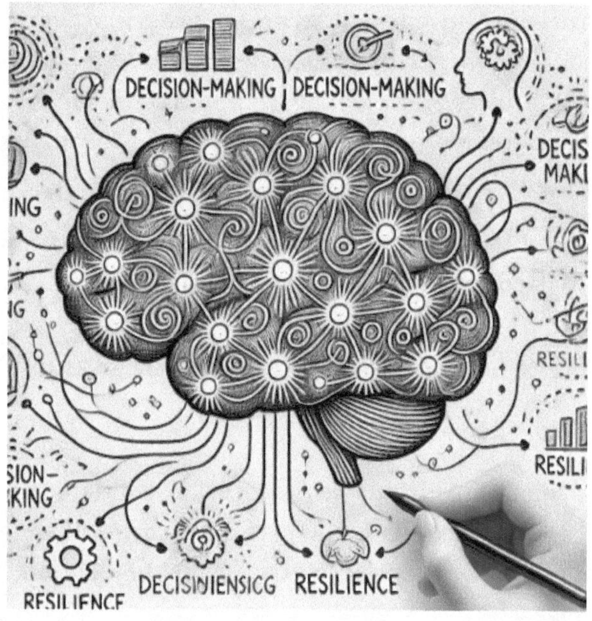

The Window of Risk and Reward

Between 18 and 25, you experience a unique intersection of freedom and responsibility:

1. Freedom:

You can explore careers, travel, build relationships, or take risks.

2. Responsibility:

You're also making financial, personal, and professional decisions that will shape your future.

"The actions you take now are like seeds planted in fertile soil. They'll grow into the habits and outcomes of your 30s, 40s, and beyond."

2. Why These Years Are Unique

A Time of Firsts

Think about the milestones you're likely to experience:

1. Your first full-time job.
2. Your first apartment.
3. Your first major failure—and your first big comeback.

Each "first" teaches you lessons that prepare you for the next stage of life.

Real-World Example:

Take Oprah Winfrey. At 22, she was fired from her first TV job for being "too emotional". Instead of giving up, she used the experience to refine her skills. By 25, she had become a rising star in television, laying the groundwork for her legendary career.

The Freedom to Fail

Unlike later in life, failure in your early twenties doesn't carry the same long-term consequences.

1. Want to start a business? Now's the time.
2. Interested in changing careers? You can pivot without significant financial or personal risk.

Action Point:

Write down three things you're afraid to try because of the fear of failure. Then, next to each one, list the potential lessons you could learn if you failed.

3. Common Pitfalls: Don't Waste These Years

The Comfort Trap

It's easy to settle into routines that feel safe but don't push you to grow.

- Spending hours scrolling social media.
- Avoiding challenges because they seem too hard.

How to Avoid This:

- Set small, challenging goals.
- Create routines that prioritise growth, like reading, networking, or exercising.

The Postponement Problem

Many people think, "I'll get serious later." However, postponing key decisions can lead to regret and missed opportunities.

Real-World Example:

Consider Jeff Bezos. In his early twenties, Bezos was already thinking about the future. By age 25, he was laying the groundwork for Amazon, the company that would define his life's work.

4. The Ripple Effect of Your Choices

Habits Compound Over Time

1. The small habits you build now—waking up early, saving money, networking—will grow exponentially.
2. Conversely, poor habits like procrastination or excessive spending can have long-term consequences.

"Every choice you make now is like a stone dropped in water. The ripples will extend far beyond what you can see today."

Action Point:

Track your habits for a week. Note which ones align with your goals and which might hold you back.

5. Real-World Examples of Transformative 1825 Stories

Malala Yousafzai

At 18, Malala became the youngest Nobel laureate, proving that passion and determination can create global change.

Elon Musk

By 24, Musk had launched his first company, Zip2, setting the stage for Tesla and SpaceX.

Serena Williams

Serena won her first Grand Slam at 17. By 25, she had revolutionised tennis, demonstrating the power of discipline and resilience.

6. Reflection: Where Are You Now?

Activity:

1. Draw a line dividing your current goals into short-term (1–2 years) and long-term (3–7 years).
2. Identify one action you can take today to move closer to each goal.

Conclusion: The Journey Begins

The years between 18 and 25 are a gift. Use them to explore, take risks, and build the habits that will carry you through life. Remember, this isn't a time to aim for perfection; it's a time to aim for progress.

CHAPTER 2

Defining Your Vision

Introduction: Turning Dreams into Reality

Have you ever stood before a blank canvas, unsure what to paint? Life between 18 and 25 often feels like excitement and uncertainty, with endless possibilities stretching out before you. But the difference between a blank canvas and a masterpiece is **vision**.

Vision is what turns ideas into action, aspirations into achievements, and confusion into clarity. Imagine Michelangelo staring at a block of marble, already seeing the statue of David within. That's what a strong vision does—it allows you to see what others can't yet, guiding you as you carve your life from raw potential.

Story: "At 24, Steve Jobs envisioned a world where personal computers weren't just tools for professionals but everyday companions for everyone. This vision led to the creation of the Apple Macintosh—a product that revolutionised technology. Jobs didn't know exactly how he'd achieve it, but his clarity about what he wanted to create gave him the focus and determination to make it real."

In this chapter, you'll learn how to craft a vision so compelling it pulls you forward, even on the hardest days.

1. What is a Vision?

A Vision is a Story of Your Future

Think of your vision as the movie trailer for your ideal life. It's not just about what you want to achieve—it's about who you want to become.

1. Why a Vision is Essential:

1. **It provides direction:** Without a vision, life can feel aimless. With one, every step has a purpose.
2. **It builds resilience:** When challenges arise, a clear vision reminds you why you started.
3. **It inspires others:** A strong vision doesn't just motivate you; it can rally friends, mentors, and even strangers to support your journey.

Vision vs. Goals

It's important to understand the distinction:

1. **Vision:** The big picture—the destination.
2. **Goals:** The specific milestones along the way.

Example:

Vision: "I want to create a global community that empowers young women."

Goals: "Host five workshops in my city this year," or "Launch a website within six months."

2. The Power of Visualisation

Why Visualisation Works

The human brain is wired to respond to vivid images. When you visualise your future, your brain interprets it as real, activating the same neural pathways as if you were already living it. This strengthens your belief and motivation.

How to Visualise Effectively

1. Find a quiet place. Close your eyes and imagine your ideal life.
2. Picture it in detail: What do you see, hear, smell, and feel?
3. Focus on the emotions: excitement, pride, contentment.

Tip: Do this daily. Over time, your vision will feel more tangible and achievable.

Story: Olympic athletes often use visualisation to prepare for competitions. Michael Phelps, for example, would mentally rehearse every stroke of his races, down to the moment he touched the wall. This practice gave him a mental edge, helping him win 28 Olympic medals.

3. Crafting Your Personal Vision: A Step-by-Step Process

Step 1: Imagine the Big Picture

Think about your life in five years. Where are you? Who are you with? What's your day like on a daily basis?

1. **Exercise:** Write a "day in the life" narrative set five years from now. Include details about your career, relationships, health, and hobbies.

Step 2: Identify Your Passions and Talents

1. **Exercise:** List five things you're passionate about and five things you're good at. Look for overlap.
2. **Example:** If you're passionate about storytelling and skilled at writing, your vision might involve becoming an author or content creator.

Step 3: Align Your Vision with Your Values

Your vision should reflect your deepest values.

1. **Exercise:** Write down your top three values (e.g., freedom, creativity, family). Then describe how your vision aligns with each one.

Step 4: Write Your Vision Statement

Condense your vision into a powerful one-paragraph statement.

1. **Example:** "In five years, I see myself as a successful graphic designer, working with clients who inspire me. I live in a vibrant city, surrounded by a supportive community, and I feel creatively fulfilled every day."

4. Real-World Visionaries and Their Lessons

J.K. Rowling: A Vision Beyond Adversity

At 25, Rowling was a single mother living on welfare. But she had a vision: a boy wizard named Harry Potter. That vision kept her writing, even when publishers rejected her manuscript. Today, her books have sold over 500 million copies.

Lesson: Your vision doesn't have to be perfect; it just has to inspire you to keep going.

Jeff Bezos: A Vision of E-Commerce

Bezos didn't just want to sell books online – he envisioned a platform where people could buy anything. His clarity and focus led to the creation of Amazon, the world's largest online retailer.

Lesson: Start with a specific goal, but keep the bigger picture in mind.

5. Overcoming Visioning Challenges

Challenge 1: Fear of Dreaming Big

1. **Solution:** Start small. Imagine one part of your ideal life, then expand as you gain clarity.

Challenge 2: Feeling Overwhelmed

1. **Solution:** Break your vision into manageable steps. Focus on progress, not perfection.

Challenge 3: Lack of Clarity

1. **Solution:** Explore. Try new activities, meet different people, and reflect on what excites you.

6. Turning Vision into Reality

Create SMART Goals

Turn your vision into actionable steps using the SMART framework:

1. **Specific:** What exactly do you want?
2. **Measurable:** How will you track progress?
3. **Achievable:** Is it realistic?
4. **Relevant:** Does it align with your vision?
5. **Time-bound:** When will you achieve it?

Build Momentum with Daily Habits.

Big visions are built on small, consistent actions.

1. Vision: Run a marathon.
2. Habit: Run 3 miles, 3 times a week.

7. Exercises After Chapter 2

Exercise 1: The Day-in-the-Life Reflection

Write a detailed description of your ideal day five years from now. Include everything—from your morning routine to your evening activities.

Exercise 2: Create Your Vision Board

1. Gather magazines, printouts, or digital tools.
2. Choose images, words, and quotes that represent your vision.
3. Arrange them into categories (e.g., career, health, relationships).

Exercise 3: Set Your First SMART Goal

Pick one part of your vision and create a SMART goal for it. Write it down and track your progress over the next month.

Conclusion: Start Today

Your vision is the blueprint for your future. The clearer it is, the easier it becomes to take the first step. Remember, every great achievement begins with someone daring to dream. Now, it's your turn.

CHAPTER 3

Understanding the Framework

The Blueprint for Achieving Your Goals

Introduction: Why Frameworks Matter

Picture this: You're standing at the base of a towering mountain. The summit represents your goals—your dream career, fulfilling relationships, financial independence, and personal growth. But without a clear path, the climb seems impossible. That's where a framework comes in.

Frameworks aren't just tools; they're your guideposts. They show you where to focus, what steps to take, and how to overcome obstacles. This chapter introduces the **1825 Framework**, a powerful system designed to help you navigate the most transformative years of your life with purpose and clarity.

Story: "When 19-year-old Michelle started her first semester at university, she was overwhelmed. Between classes, a part-time job, and managing her finances, she felt like she was treading water. Then, a mentor introduced her to a goal-setting framework. For the first time, Michelle had a structure to organise her life. By 23, she graduated at the top of her class, started her dream job, and even launched a side hustle. She credits her success to having a clear system."

1. What is a Framework?

The Role of a Framework in Success

A framework is a structured approach to achieving your goals. It's like the scaffolding builders use to construct skyscrapers—without it, even the best plans can collapse.

1. Why Frameworks Work:

1. They provide clarity and focus.
2. They break big goals into manageable steps.
3. They make progress measurable and repeatable.

Example: Imagine baking a cake without a recipe. You might end up with a masterpiece—or a disaster. Frameworks are the recipes for success.

2. The 1825 Framework

The **1825 Framework** is built around five core pillars: **Clarity, Discipline, Resilience, Balance, and Growth Mindset.** Let's explore each one in detail.

Pillar 1: Clarity

You can't hit a target you can't see. Clarity is about defining your goals and understanding why they matter.

1. Questions to Ask Yourself:

1. What do I truly want?
2. Why is this important to me?

Story: "At 20, Brian felt stuck in a dead-end job. Then, he sat down and wrote his long-term goals: to work in tech, move to a big city, and earn a six-figure salary. Within two years, Brian completed a coding boot camp, landed his first tech job, and relocated to San Francisco—all because he started with clarity."

Pillar 2: Discipline

Discipline is the bridge between your goals and your results. It's about building habits that support consistent progress.

1. Key Practices:

1. Start small. Focus on one habit at a time.
2. Track your progress daily.

Example: Athletes like Serena Williams credit their success to relentless discipline, whether practising serves for hours or sticking to strict routines.

Pillar 3: Resilience

Life isn't a straight path. Resilience helps you adapt, recover, and grow stronger when things don't go as planned.

1. **Mantra:** "Failure isn't final—it's feedback."

Story: "Thomas Edison famously failed 1,000 times before inventing the light bulb. When asked about his failures, he said, 'I didn't fail 1,000 times. The light bulb was an invention with 1,000 steps.'"

Pillar 4: Balance

Achieving your goals shouldn't come at the cost of your well-being. Balance is about managing your time and energy across work, relationships, and self-care.

2. **Key Insight:** It's okay to rest. Productivity isn't about doing more—it's about doing what matters.

Pillar 5: Growth Mindset

Your abilities aren't fixed. With effort and learning, you can improve. A growth mindset helps you embrace challenges and see failures as opportunities.

1. **Belief:** "I can learn and grow, no matter where I start."

3. Applying the 1825 Framework to Your Life

Step 1: Set a Goal

Choose one goal you want to achieve in the next six months. Write it down in specific terms.

Step 2: Align with the Framework

1. **Clarity:** Why do you want to achieve this goal?
2. **Discipline:** What habits will help you get there?
3. **Resilience:** How will you handle setbacks?
4. **Balance:** How will you avoid burnout?
5. **Growth Mindset:** What will you learn along the way?

Step 3: Take Action

Start with one small step today. Remember, progress is better than perfection.

Story: "Maria wanted to learn graphic design but felt intimidated by the complexity of the tools. Using the 1825 Framework, she set a goal to design a poster within three months. She broke the goal into weekly habits, like watching tutorials and practising. When she struggled, she reminded herself that every expert was once a beginner. By the end of three months, Maria had not only designed a poster but also landed her first freelance gig."

4. Real-Life Success Stories with Frameworks

Mark Zuckerberg's Vision for Facebook

At 20, Zuckerberg envisioned a platform to connect the world. His clarity of purpose, discipline, and growth mindset helped him navigate the challenges of building Facebook.

Malala Yousafzai's Advocacy for Education

Malala's resilience and clarity of mission—ensuring education for girls worldwide—have driven her success as a global activist, despite facing life-threatening opposition.

5. Obstacles and How to Overcome Them

Obstacle 1: Fear of Starting

1. **Solution:** Start small. Action breeds confidence.

Obstacle 2: Lack of Motivation

1. **Solution:** Reconnect with your "why". Your vision is your source of energy.

Obstacle 3: Impatience

1. **Solution:** Trust the process. Success takes time, but every step moves you forward.

6. Exercises After Chapter 3

Exercise 1: Framework Alignment

Choose one goal and answer the following questions:

1. **Clarity:** What's your goal, and why is it important?
2. **Discipline:** What daily habits will support this goal?
3. **Resilience:** How will you handle setbacks?
4. **Balance:** How will you maintain your well-being?
5. **Growth Mindset:** What will you learn during this process?

Exercise 2: Weekly Review

At the end of each week, review your progress:

1. What worked?
2. What didn't?
3. What can you improve next week?

Exercise 3: Resilience in Action

Think of a recent failure or setback. Write down:

1. What did you learn from it?
2. How can you use this lesson to move forward?

The Story of Maya: A Framework for Transformation

At 19, Maya felt like life was slipping through her fingers. She juggled college, two part-time jobs, and an overwhelming uncertainty about her future. While her friends seemed to have everything figured out—internships, career plans, even dream vacations—Maya was stuck in a cycle of survival. Every day was the same: wake up, attend classes, work, study, and collapse into bed, only to do it all over again.

Her dreams of becoming an architect felt distant, almost impossible. Bills, grades, and burnout consumed her thoughts. It wasn't that she lacked ambition; she simply didn't know where to start.

One afternoon, Maya sat in her campus library scrolling through videos on her phone. She stumbled upon a TED Talk titled "The Power of Systems." The speaker's words resonated deeply: "Dreams are vague. Goals are specific. Systems are actionable." It was the first time Maya realised she needed more than just hope—she needed a framework.

Step 1: Clarity

The first thing Maya did was get a clarity on what she wanted. She borrowed a notebook and wrote down her dreams, starting with, "I want to become a licensed architect and design sustainable housing." Writing it felt monumental. For the first time, her dream had formed—it wasn't just a wish floating in her head.

But Maya didn't stop there. She added details:

- **Where:** "I see myself working for a firm in Chicago."
- **Why:** "I want to create affordable, eco-friendly homes that change lives."

Step 2: Discipline

Clarity wasn't enough. Maya needed habits to turn her dream into reality. She broke her big goal into smaller steps:

- Research architecture programmes.
- Apply for scholarships and internships.
- Build a strong portfolio.

She committed to studying for two hours every morning before work. It was hard at first, especially with late-night shifts, but she reminded herself of her vision. To stay accountable, she used a habit tracker, marking off every day she completed her study session.

Step 3: Resilience

One semester, Maya failed a crucial design course. Her confidence crumbled. For weeks, she questioned her abilities. Maybe architecture wasn't for her. But then she remembered the TED Talk's message about resilience: "Failures are feedback".

Instead of giving up, Maya scheduled a meeting with her professor. She learned where she went wrong and asked for guidance. The professor offered her extra resources and even connected her with a mentor in the industry. By the end of the semester, Maya had not only passed the course but gained a valuable ally.

Step 4: Balance

Maya also learned the importance of balance. She realised burnout wouldn't help her achieve her goals. She started scheduling time for herself: yoga on Saturdays, dinner with friends once a week, and an hour of journaling every night.

Step 5: Growth Mindset

Finally, Maya embraced the idea that growth comes from continuous learning. She joined an architecture club, attended workshops, and devoured books about design. She stopped fearing criticism and started seeking it out, knowing every piece of feedback would strengthen her.

By 24, Maya had graduated, landed a job at her dream firm, and completed her first sustainable housing project. She credits her transformation to the framework that helped her turn chaos into clarity.

Part II

Building Skills for Success

CHAPTER 4

Mastering Time Management

Making Every Moment Count

Introduction: The Currency of Time

Imagine that every morning, you wake up with 1,440 minutes deposited into your "time bank account". You can spend those minutes however you choose, but at the end of the day, your balance resets. You can't save them for tomorrow, and you can't earn more. The question is: How will you spend today's deposit?

Time is the great equaliser. No matter who you are or where you come from, every person gets the same 24 hours each day. Yet, some people seem to accomplish so much more than others. How? The difference lies not in the amount of time available, but in how it's managed.

Mastering time management isn't about cramming more into your schedule or sacrificing sleep to be productive. It's about working smarter, focusing on what truly matters, and finding balance to achieve your goals without burning out.

This chapter is your guide to mastering the art of time management. By the end, you'll not only understand the principles and strategies of effective time management but also feel inspired to take control of your day.

The Story of Sarah: From Overwhelmed to Empowered

At 21, Sarah felt like her life was spiralling out of control. A full-time college student with a part-time job and a volunteer position at a local nonprofit, she was constantly running from one obligation to the next. Her grades started slipping, her relationships felt strained, and her health was deteriorating from stress and sleepless nights.

"I just don't have enough time," she told her mentor during a lunch meeting one afternoon. "I'm doing so much, but it feels like I'm accomplishing nothing."

Her mentor smiled knowingly. "Sarah," he said, "Time isn't the issue. The problem is how you're using it. Let me show you something."

He pulled out a piece of paper and drew a simple grid with four quadrants, labelling them:

1. **Urgent and Important**
2. **Not Urgent but Important**
3. **Urgent but Not Important**
4. **Not Urgent and Not Important**

"This is called the Eisenhower Matrix," he explained. "The trick to time management is spending most of your energy on the second quadrant: things that are important but not urgent. That's where real growth happens. When you ignore this quadrant, everything piles up until it becomes urgent, and that's when you feel overwhelmed."

Over the next few weeks, Sarah started applying the matrix to her daily life. She scheduled study sessions before exams became urgent, prioritised her health by planning workouts, and cut back on non-essential tasks. She even started time-blocking her days, dedicating specific hours to focused work and relaxation.

Within a semester, Sarah's grades improved, her stress levels dropped, and she even found time to start painting again—a hobby she'd abandoned years earlier. For Sarah, mastering time management wasn't about doing more; it was about doing what mattered most.

1. The Value of Time: Understanding Its True Cost

Why Time Feels Scarce

Time feels scarce when we don't manage it well. Procrastination, distractions, and a lack of prioritisation can leave us feeling like there aren't enough hours in the day. The truth is that most of us waste more time than we realise.

1. **Reflection:** Think about the last week. How many hours did you spend scrolling through social media, binge-watching TV, or aimlessly browsing the internet? Now imagine redirecting just half of that time towards something meaningful.

The Irreplaceable Nature of Time

Time is unique because it's irreplaceable. You can earn back lost money, rebuild broken relationships, or regain your health, but time once spent is gone forever.

Example: Bill Gates and Elon Musk have the same 24 hours as you. Their secret? Ruthlessly prioritising tasks that align with their long-term goals.

Every hour wasted on distractions is an hour you could have spent building your future, connecting with loved ones, or taking care of yourself. Recognising this truth is the first step towards valuing your time.

2. The Core Principles of Time Management

Mastering time management starts with understanding its core principles: prioritisation, focus, scheduling, and efficiency.

Principle 1: Prioritisation

Not all tasks are created equal. Some will have a significant impact on your goals, while others are merely distractions disguised as obligations. The key is to focus on what truly matters.

1. Tool: The Eisenhower Matrix.

1. **Quadrant 1: Urgent and Important** (e.g., meeting deadlines, handling emergencies).
2. **Quadrant 2: Not Urgent but Important** (e.g., planning, personal growth, relationship-building).
3. **Quadrant 3: Urgent but Not Important** (e.g., responding to non-critical emails).
4. **Quadrant 4: Not Urgent and Not Important** (e.g. excessive social media use, mindless TV).

Key Insight: Spend most of your energy in Quadrant 2. This is where long-term success is built.

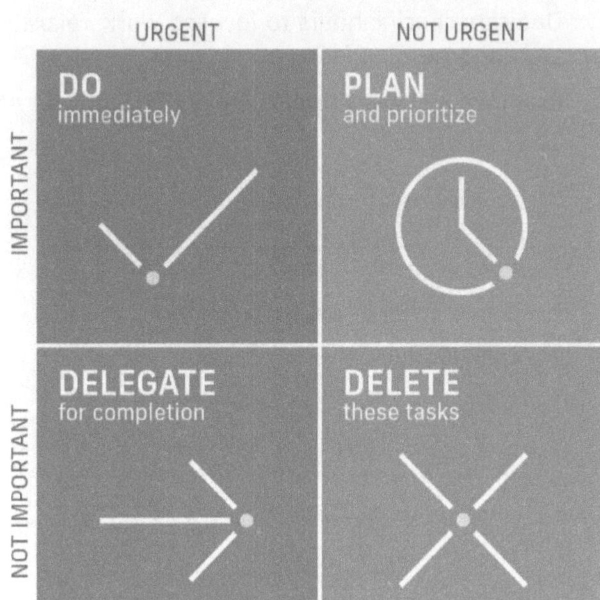

Principle 2: The Power of Focus

Multitasking is a myth. Studies show that switching between tasks reduces productivity by up to 40%. Instead, focus on one task at a time for maximum efficiency.

1. **Tip:** Use the Pomodoro Technique: Work for 25 minutes, then take a 5-minute break. Repeat this cycle four times, then take a longer break.

Principle 3: Scheduling Over Lists

To-do lists are a great starting point, but they don't ensure that tasks get done. Scheduling your tasks into specific time slots makes them actionable.

1. Tool: Time Blocking

1. Dedicate specific hours to focused work, relaxation, and self-care.
2. Example: 8–9 AM: Exercise, 9–11 AM: Study, 11 AM–12 PM: Emails.

Principle 4: The 80/20 Rule

The Pareto Principle states that 80% of your results come from 20% of your efforts. Identify and prioritise the 20% of tasks that have the greatest impact.

Reflection: Ask yourself, "What are the few tasks that, if completed, will make everything else easier or unnecessary?"

3. Real-Life Strategies for Mastering Time

Strategy 1: The Morning Power Hour

Start your day with intention. Dedicate the first hour to high-impact activities like planning, exercising, or learning.

Story: Benjamin Franklin's morning routine included asking himself, "What good shall I do today?" This daily reflection helped him focus on meaningful actions.

Strategy 2: Batch Similar Tasks

Group similar tasks together to save time and mental energy. For example:

1. Answer all emails in one time block instead of sporadically throughout the day.
2. Cook meals for the week in one session to avoid daily meal prep.

Strategy 3: Eliminate Time Thieves

Identify and minimise activities that steal your time. Common time thieves include:

1. Checking your phone every 10 minutes.
2. Saying yes to tasks or events that don't align with your priorities.

Tip: Use apps like Freedom or Forest to block distractions and stay focused.

4. Overcoming Obstacles to Time Management

Obstacle 1: Procrastination

Procrastination often stems from fear of failure or feeling overwhelmed by large tasks.

1. **Solution:** Break tasks into smaller, manageable steps. Start with just five minutes to build momentum.

Obstacle 2: Overcommitment

Saying yes to everything spreads you too thin, leaving little time for what matters most.

- **Solution:** Practice saying no to tasks or events that don't align with your priorities.

Obstacle 3: Distractions

From social media notifications to cluttered workspaces, distractions can derail your focus.

- **Solution:** Create a distraction-free environment. Turn off notifications, clear your workspace, and set boundaries with others.

The Case Studies: Time Management in Action

Case Study 1: Lisa – From Overcommitted to Organised

Lisa was a 22-year-old marketing student working two part-time jobs. Her planner was bursting with commitments: group projects, internship tasks, social events, and family obligations. She said yes to everything, thinking staying busy was the key to success. But she felt like she was constantly treading water.

The Turning Point:

One day, her professor introduced her to the Pareto Principle, also known as the 80/20 Rule. She learned that 80% of her results likely came from 20% of her efforts. Lisa started identifying the tasks that had the most impact on her grades, career, and personal life.

1. She delegated low-priority tasks to her teammates.
2. She politely declined social invites that didn't align with her goals.
3. She focused on her top priorities: preparing for a major internship presentation and acing her final project.

Within weeks, Lisa's stress levels dropped, and her productivity skyrocketed. By focusing on fewer, more meaningful activities, she excelled in her studies and impressed her internship supervisor, leading to a full-time job offer.

Key Takeaway: Less is more. Focus on the tasks that deliver the biggest impact.

Case Study 2: Raj – Overcoming Procrastination

Raj was a 20-year-old engineering student with big dreams of starting his own tech company. But he had one major problem: procrastination. He often delayed important assignments until the last minute, leaving him stressed and sleep-deprived.

The Turning Point:

During a campus workshop, Raj learned about the Pomodoro Technique, a time management method in which one works for 25 minutes and then takes a 5-minute break. The concept sounded simple, but Raj decided to give it a try.

1. He started by setting a timer for 25 minutes and focusing on a single task.
2. During breaks, he rewarded himself with a quick walk or a snack.
3. Over time, his focus and productivity improved, and he no longer dreaded starting big tasks.

By the end of the semester, Raj not only completed his assignments on time but also built a prototype for his first app, a project he had been procrastinating on for months.

Key Takeaway: Break tasks into manageable chunks and use small rewards to stay motivated.

Case Study 3: Maria – Balancing Work and Life

Maria, a 24-year-old nurse, worked long shifts at a busy hospital. Her demanding job left her exhausted, and she struggled to find time for her personal life. She wanted to start a fitness routine, reconnect with friends, and pursue her love for painting, but every day felt like a race against the clock.

The Turning Point:

Maria discovered the power of time blocking, a method where you schedule specific activities into your calendar.

1. She blocked out an hour each morning for exercise, treating it as a non-negotiable appointment.
2. She dedicated Friday evenings to catching up with friends and Sunday afternoons to painting.

3. She used her commute to listen to audiobooks, turning idle time into learning opportunities.

Within months, Maria felt more balanced and fulfilled. Her energy levels improved, her relationships strengthened, and she even completed a painting that won a local art competition.

Key Takeaway: Time blocking helps you make time for the things that matter most.

Case Study 4: James – Managing Distractions

James, a 19-year-old aspiring writer, struggled with staying focused. Every time he sat down to write, his phone buzzed with notifications, or he'd find himself scrolling through social media. Hours would slip away without any meaningful progress.

The Turning Point:

Frustrated by his lack of productivity, James downloaded an app called Freedom, which blocks distracting websites and apps during scheduled periods.

1. He started with 90-minute focus blocks where he'd write without interruptions.
2. He turned off all non-essential notifications on his phone and laptop.
3. He created a "distraction-free zone" by keeping his workspace clean and setting clear boundaries with roommates.

Over the next six months, James wrote and published his first collection of short stories. His ability to eliminate distractions not only improved his writing, but also gave him more time for relaxation and self-care.

Key Takeaway: Eliminate distractions to create a focused environment for deep work.

Case Study 5: Priya – Finding Purpose in the Chaos

Priya, a 23-year-old entrepreneur, had a growing e-commerce business but felt overwhelmed by the demands of running it. She juggled everything herself—inventory, customer service, marketing—and worked late into the night, only to wake up feeling drained and anxious.

The Turning Point:

Priya's mentor encouraged her to use the Eisenhower Matrix to categorise her tasks and focus on the important ones.

1. She outsourced repetitive tasks, like inventory management, to a virtual assistant.
2. She focused her energy on high-impact activities like building partnerships and launching new products.
3. She scheduled "CEO Time" every Friday to strategise and plan for the future.

By focusing on what truly mattered, Priya doubled her revenue in a year and finally had time to enjoy the fruits of her labour.

Key Takeaway: Delegating and prioritising high-impact tasks can transform how you work.

5. Exercises After Chapter 4

Exercise 1: The Weekly Time Audit

Track how you spend your time for one week. Categorise activities into productive, neutral, or wasteful. At the end of the week:

1. Identify time-wasting activities.
2. Plan how to redirect that time towards your goals.

Exercise 2: Create Your Perfect Day

Design an ideal schedule for a typical day using time blocking. Include time for work, rest, and personal growth. Be realistic but intentional.

Exercise 3: The One-Thing Challenge

Each morning, ask yourself: "What's the one thing I can do today that will make everything else easier or unnecessary?" Focus on completing that task first.

Conclusion: Time is Your Most Valuable Asset

Time is finite, but its potential is infinite. By mastering the art of time management, you can take control of your day and design a life that aligns with your values and goals. Remember, every minute is an opportunity to create, learn, and grow.

It's time to reclaim your 1,440 minutes. How will you spend them?

CHAPTER 5

Developing Self-Discipline

Mastering the Art of Consistency, Commitment, and Perseverance

Why This Chapter Matters

When we think about success, we often imagine passion, talent, or even luck as the driving forces. While those elements can play a role, the real game-changer is **self-discipline**. It is the engine that powers consistent effort, deliberate practice, and focused determination. Without discipline, even the most talented individuals can flounder. With it, ordinary people can achieve extraordinary things.

Self-discipline is not just about saying "no" to distractions; it's about saying "yes" to the life you want to create. This chapter focuses on helping you understand the science, strategies, and stories behind the discipline and how to weave it into the fabric of your life.

Quote: "We must all suffer one of two things: the pain of discipline or the pain of regret." – Jim Rohn

What is Self-Discipline?

Self-discipline is the ability to do what needs to be done, even when you don't feel like doing it. It's about aligning your actions with your long-term goals, despite temptations or discomfort. Think of it as the invisible force that pushes you to study instead of binge-watching Netflix, to wake up early for a run instead of hitting snooze, or to save money instead of overspending.

The Three Core Pillars of Self-Discipline

1. Commitment:

Commitment is the unwavering promise you make to yourself to stay the course, regardless of challenges or setbacks. It's the fuel that drives action.

1. **Example:** A college student committed to graduating with honours sacrifices weekends to study and refuses to let procrastination derail their plans.

2. Consistency:

Success doesn't come from one-off efforts. It's the cumulative effect of small, deliberate actions repeated every single day. Consistency ensures that progress, no matter how small, keeps building over time.

1. **Example:** A writer who dedicates 30 minutes a day to writing will have a completed manuscript in less than a year.

3. Resilience:

1. Resilience is what keeps you going when things don't go as planned. It's the ability to bounce back, learn from failures, and keep striving.

1. **Example:** A runner training for a marathon misses a week due to illness but returns to their routine with renewed focus, refusing to give up on their goal.

Why Self-Discipline is Crucial for Success

The Role of Habits

Habits are the building blocks of self-discipline. They automate behaviour, making it easier to act without relying on willpower. Discipline helps you create habits that align with your goals, whether exercising regularly, sticking to a study schedule, or saving money.

Example: Kobe Bryant's habit of starting his day at 4 a.m. for intense practice sessions wasn't an occasional effort but a routine that built his legacy.

The Struggle Against Instant Gratification

We live in an age of instant gratification. Social media, streaming platforms, and fast food have trained us to expect immediate rewards. Discipline counters this by teaching us to delay short-term pleasures for long-term gains.

Insight: Every time you choose to delay gratification—like studying instead of scrolling through Instagram—you strengthen your ability to focus on what truly matters.

Discipline Creates Freedom

At first, discipline might feel restrictive. But over time, it provides freedom—the freedom to achieve your goals, live with purpose, and create a life that aligns with your dreams.

Key Insight: Discipline is liberating. It frees you from the chaos of procrastination and the burden of unfulfilled potential.

The Science of Self-Discipline

How Habits Rewire the Brain

Your brain is constantly reshaping itself based on your behaviours, a concept known as **neuroplasticity**. When you repeat a behaviour, you strengthen the neural pathways associated with it. Over time, these pathways become automatic, turning effort into habit.

Example: If you consistently wake up early to exercise, your brain adapts, and the behaviour becomes second nature.

The Dopamine Effect

Dopamine is a neurotransmitter responsible for the brain's reward system. Achieving small milestones releases dopamine, reinforcing positive behaviour. Breaking larger goals into smaller, achievable steps creates a steady flow of dopamine, making discipline more sustainable.

Example: Completing a short workout triggers a dopamine release, motivating you to repeat the habit the next day.

Case Studies: Self-Discipline in Action

Case Study 1: Kobe Bryant – The Relentless Pursuit of Greatness

Kobe Bryant's discipline was legendary. Known for his 4 am practice sessions, Kobe believed that hard work and consistency were non-negotiable. During a Team USA training camp, Kobe invited his trainer for an early-morning session. When the trainer arrived, Kobe had already been practising for an hour.

This relentless commitment wasn't occasional; it was a lifestyle. Kobe often said:

"I don't understand lazy people. We don't speak the same language."

Key Takeaway: Success is built on the foundation of disciplined effort, repeated daily.

Case Study 2: J.K. Rowling – Writing Through Hardship

Before *Harry Potter* became a global phenomenon, J.K. Rowling faced severe challenges. As a single mother living on welfare, she could have given up on her dream of writing. Instead, she disciplined herself to write daily, even if it was only for a short time.

Despite being rejected by 12 publishers, Rowling persisted. Her discipline turned her manuscript into one of the most beloved series of all time.

Key Takeaway: Discipline helps you push through adversity and turn your dreams into reality.

Case Study 3: The British Cycling Team – Marginal Gains

The British Cycling team was struggling until a new coach introduced the concept of "marginal gains". The team focused on improving every aspect of performance by just 1%—bike designs, training methods, and even sleep quality.

These small, disciplined changes compounded over time, leading to massive success. By the 2008 Olympics, the team dominated the competition, winning eight gold medals.

Key Takeaway: Even small, disciplined efforts can create extraordinary results over time.

Practical Strategies for Building Self-Discipline

1. Start Small

Discipline doesn't mean overhauling your entire life overnight. Start with manageable goals to build momentum.

Example: If you want to exercise regularly, begin with 10-minute walks instead of committing to hour-long workouts.

2. Use the Two-Minute Rule

The hardest part of any task is starting. The two-minute rule encourages you to commit to just two minutes of effort.

Example: Want to write a book? Commit to writing one sentence a day.

3. Design Your Environment

Remove temptations and create an environment that supports your goals.

Example: If you want to study, keep your workspace clean, turn off notifications, and set specific times for breaks.

4. Track Your Progress

Use a habit tracker to monitor your consistency. Seeing your progress builds motivation.

Example: Marking off each day you complete a habit creates a sense of accomplishment.

5. Reward Yourself

Celebrating small wins keeps you motivated and reinforces positive behaviour.

Example: Treat yourself to a favourite activity after a week of consistent effort.

Exercises to Cultivate Self-Discipline

Exercise 1: Build a Habit Tracker

Create a habit tracker for 30 days. Choose one habit and commit to it daily, marking off each day you succeed. Reflect on your progress at the end of the month.

Exercise 2: The 1% Improvement Plan

Identify one area you want to improve. Break it into small, actionable steps and track your progress. Focus on improving just 1 percent every day.

Exercise 3: Visualise Your Success

Write a detailed description of how your life will look in one year if you practice self-discipline consistently. Include specifics about your goals, routines, and feelings.

Conclusion: Discipline is the Key to Freedom

Self-discipline is the invisible force behind every success story. It empowers you to overcome challenges, delay gratification, and stay consistent in the pursuit of your goals.

Quote: "The difference between who you are and who you want to be is what you do." – Unknown

Start small. Stay consistent. Embrace the journey. Let discipline become the foundation of the life you want to build.

CHAPTER 6

Building Meaningful Relationships

The Art and Science of Connection

Why This Chapter Matters

Imagine a world without connections—no friends to laugh with, no mentors to guide you, and no loved ones to share your triumphs. Relationships are the threads that weave the fabric of our lives, yet many people struggle to build and maintain them.

This chapter is your roadmap to creating meaningful, lasting relationships in every aspect of life—personal, professional, and romantic. Whether it's learning how to resolve conflicts, mastering the art of empathy, or building a strong network, this guide will arm you with the tools to connect deeply with others while staying true to yourself.

Quote: "Connection is why we're here. It's what gives purpose and meaning to our lives." – Brené Brown.

A Journey Through the Science of Relationships

Relationships aren't just social constructs; they are deeply rooted in our biology. Let's explore the neuroscience, evolutionary psychology, and sociology that underpin our desire for connection.

1. The Evolutionary Need for Connection

1. **Tribal Survival:** Our ancestors depended on social groups for survival. From hunting to protection, cooperation was the key to thriving.
2. **Biological Bonds:** Oxytocin, often called the "love hormone", strengthens bonds between humans, reinforcing trust and intimacy.

Example: Studies show that oxytocin levels increase when people hug, fostering feelings of connection and well-being.

2. The Role of Mirror Neurons in Empathy

Mirror neurons in our brains activate when we observe others' emotions or actions, allowing us to understand and empathise with them.

- **Practical Insight:** Developing empathy is like training a muscle. The more you practice understanding others' perspectives, the stronger your connections become.

3. Sociology of Social Networks

- **Strong Ties vs. Weak Ties:** Sociologist Mark Granovetter's research shows that "weak ties" (acquaintances) are often more valuable for career opportunities than "strong ties" (close friends).

- **Social Capital:** The resources and support we gain from our networks enrich our lives in countless ways.

Deep Dive into the Pillars of Meaningful Relationships

1. Trust: The Bedrock of Connection

Trust is earned through consistent behaviour, transparency, and reliability. Without trust, relationships are built on shaky ground.

1. Building Trust:

1. Be dependable: Follow through on your promises.
2. Practice vulnerability: Share your fears and dreams to deepen bonds.
3. Avoid gossip: Protect others' confidentiality to establish integrity.

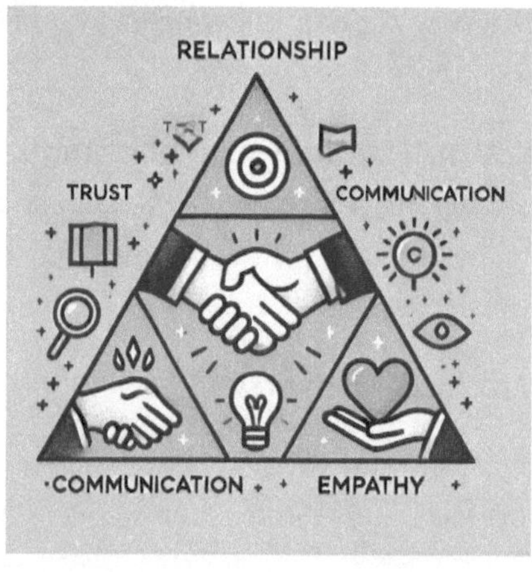

2. Communication: The Lifeline of Relationships

Clear, honest, and respectful communication prevents misunderstandings and fosters connection.

1. Techniques for Better Communication:

1. **Active Listening:** Fully focus on what the other person is saying without planning your response.
2. **Nonviolent Communication:** Use "I" statements to express feelings and needs without blame.
3. **Reflective Responses:** Paraphrase what the other person has said to show understanding.

Quote: "The most important thing in communication is hearing what isn't said." – Peter Drucker

3. Empathy: Walking in Someone Else's Shoes

Empathy transforms ordinary interactions into meaningful connections. It's about feeling with someone, not just for them.

1. Developing Empathy:

1. Ask open-ended questions: "How did that make you feel?"
2. Imagine their perspective: Visualise the situation from their point of view.
3. Practice mindfulness: Stay present during conversations.

Activity Break: Reflect on a recent disagreement. Write down how the other person might have felt and what you could have done to better understand their perspective.

Case Studies: Real-Life Lessons in Relationships

Case Study 1: Oprah and Gayle – A Friendship for the Ages

Oprah Winfrey and Gayle King have one of the most iconic friendships in modern history. Their bond, which began when they worked together at a local TV station, has spanned decades of personal and professional highs and lows.

How it all began:

In the late 1970s, Oprah and Gayle were young women starting in the world of broadcasting. One evening, a snowstorm trapped them at Oprah's house. They spent the night talking and sharing their dreams and fears. This unexpected sleepover became the foundation of a lifelong friendship rooted in vulnerability and honesty.

Challenges They Faced:

Both women faced immense scrutiny as Oprah's fame skyrocketed. Media rumours and gossip tested their bond, but their trust and mutual respect never wavered. Instead of succumbing to the pressures of the spotlight, they supported one another.

What Makes Their Friendship Strong:

1. Authenticity: They can be completely themselves around each other, without fear of judgment.
2. Unwavering Support: Oprah credits Gayle with helping her navigate the challenges of fame, while

    Gayle acknowledges how Oprah's encouragement has shaped her career.

3. Celebrating Success Together: Despite Oprah's larger-than-life persona, she never overshadowed Gayle. They celebrate each other's achievements equally.

Key Takeaway: True friendships thrive on trust, honesty, and the ability to support one another through life's ups and downs.

Case Study 2: Michelle's Mentor – One Coffee, Endless Impact

Michelle was a 22-year-old college graduate overwhelmed by the thought of starting her career. With no idea where to begin, she took a bold step: she reached out to an alumnus she admired on LinkedIn, asking for a 15-minute coffee chat.

How It Happened:

The alumna, Lisa, responded warmly. During their meeting, Michelle asked thoughtful questions about Lisa's career journey and shared her own aspirations. Lisa was impressed by Michelle's enthusiasm and offered to stay in touch.

The Impact of Mentorship:

Over the next year, Lisa became Michelle's unofficial mentor. She provided:

1. Career Guidance: Lisa helped Michelle refine her resume and prepare for interviews.

2. Industry Insights: Lisa shared insider tips about the job market, helping Michelle stand out as a candidate.
3. Networking Opportunities: Lisa introduced Michelle to other professionals, opening doors to new opportunities.

Michelle eventually landed a role at a top company, a job she credits to the insights and connections Lisa provided.

What Made This Work:

1. Michelle approached Lisa with respect and gratitude, making her feel valued.
2. Lisa was generous with her time and genuinely invested in Michelle's growth.
3. Their relationship was mutually beneficial—Lisa found fulfilment in helping a rising star, while Michelle gained invaluable guidance.

Key Takeaway: Building meaningful professional relationships starts with one courageous step. Don't be afraid to reach out and ask for guidance.

Case Study 3: Raj's Start-Up – Listening as a Superpower

Raj was a 25-year-old entrepreneur excited to launch his tech start-up. His idea was innovative, and he worked tirelessly to bring it to life. However, after the first year, he faced a major problem: employees were leaving at an alarming rate. Frustrated and unsure of what to do, Raj sought advice from a mentor who suggested that the issue might lie in his leadership style.

The Problem:

Raj realised he wasn't truly listening to his team. Employees felt overworked and undervalued, but Raj was too focused on scaling the business to notice.

The Solution:

Raj implemented a weekly one-on-one meeting with each employee. During these sessions, he asked:

1. "What's one thing we can do to make your job better?"
2. "What challenges are you facing, and how can I help?"
3. "What motivates you to stay, and what might cause you to leave?"

The Transformation:

These conversations revealed crucial insights:

1. Employees wanted clearer goals and better communication from leadership.
2. They valued flexibility and recognition for their contributions.
3. Small changes, like updating tools and improving team collaboration, made a big difference.

Raj acted on this feedback, and the results were remarkable: turnover dropped by 50%, productivity increased, and the team's morale improved. Employees felt heard, valued, and motivated to contribute to the company's success.

Key Takeaway: Active listening isn't just a nice-to-have; it's a superpower that transforms relationships. When people feel heard, they're more likely to stay engaged and committed.

Case Study 4: Lisa's Friendship Revival – The Courage to Apologise

Lisa and her best friend Maya had been inseparable for years. However, one heated argument about a miscommunication during a group project left them angry and estranged. Months passed, and though both missed each other, neither wanted to make the first move.

The Turning Point:

One day, Lisa realised she valued their friendship more than her pride. She sent Maya a simple text: "I miss you. Can we talk?"

Maya responded immediately, agreeing to meet. During their conversation, Lisa apologised for her part in the argument and expressed how much their friendship meant to her. Maya reciprocated, and they both acknowledged their mistakes.

How They Rebuilt Their Bond:

1. They committed to being more open and honest with each other.
2. They learned to give each other grace during disagreements.
3. They focused on creating positive memories to rebuild trust.

Today, Lisa and Maya's friendship is stronger than ever. The argument that once drove them apart is now a lesson they often laugh about.

Key Takeaway: Apologies are powerful. They take courage but can heal wounds and pave the way for even stronger connections.

Case Study 5: The Wright Brothers – Repairing a Professional Bond

Orville and Wilbur Wright are celebrated as the pioneers of modern aviation. But behind their historic achievements lay a complex sibling relationship filled with collaboration, rivalry, and even estrangement.

The Conflict:

As their aviation business grew, disagreements about its direction strained their partnership. At one point, the brothers stopped speaking to each other for months.

The Reconciliation:

Realising that their shared vision was more important than their differences, Orville and Wilbur made amends. They redefined their roles within the business to minimise conflict and focused on their strengths.

The Result:

Their renewed partnership led to further innovations in aviation, cementing their legacy as pioneers who shaped history.

Key Takeaway: Even deeply strained relationships can be repaired when both parties are willing to compromise and prioritise shared goals.

Lessons from the Case Studies.

These stories illustrate that meaningful relationships—whether personal, professional, or familial—require effort, empathy, and intentionality. They remind us that:

1. A single conversation can spark a life-changing connection.
2. Listening and vulnerability are the foundations of trust.
3. Conflicts, when handled with care, can lead to growth and stronger bonds.

Strategies for Building and Strengthening Relationships

Let's dive deeper into the strategies for cultivating and maintaining meaningful relationships. Each strategy will include actionable steps, real-life examples, and nuanced insights to help you not only understand but apply these principles in your life.

1. Prioritise Quality Over Quantity

Many people believe that having a large social circle is a sign of success. However, research and real-world experience show that the depth of your connections matters far more than their number. It's the meaningful relationships that truly enrich your life.

1. Why This Matters:

1. Superficial relationships often lack the trust and understanding necessary to provide genuine support.
2. Deep relationships foster emotional security, mutual growth, and long-lasting fulfilment.

2. How to Apply This Strategy:

1. Identify Your Core Circle: Reflect on the people who make you feel valued, supported, and understood. Prioritise nurturing these connections.
2. Invest Time and Energy: Spend quality time with a few close friends or family members rather than spreading yourself too thin across a larger group.
3. Be Selective: Choose relationships that align with your values and goals, and let go of connections that are consistently toxic or draining.

Example: Think of a friend who always uplifts you. Instead of attending a large social gathering, plan a one-on-one coffee date to deepen your bond.

2. Show Up Consistently

Consistency is the glue that holds relationships together. It's not grand gestures but small, regular acts of care and attention that strengthen bonds over time.

1. Why This Matters:

1. Relationships thrive on reliability and trust. Inconsistent behaviour can weaken even the strongest connections.
2. Being present during both joyful and challenging times creates a sense of security and mutual respect.

2. How to Apply This Strategy:

1. Schedule Regular Check-Ins: Make it a habit to call or text your loved ones regularly. A simple "How are you doing?" can go a long way.

2. Celebrate Important Moments: Remember birthdays, anniversaries, and other milestones.
3. Be There in Tough Times: Your presence matters most when someone is facing challenges.

Example: A colleague who always remembers your work anniversary and congratulates you is more likely to have a lasting connection than one who only speaks to you occasionally.

3. Invest in Shared Experiences

Shared experiences create memories that deepen relationships. Whether it's a simple walk, a vacation, or a collaborative project, these moments foster trust, understanding, and joy.

1. Why This Matters:

1. Experiencing things together helps create a sense of belonging and shared purpose.
2. Activities that require teamwork build mutual respect and collaboration.

2. How to Apply This Strategy:

1. Plan Activities You Both Enjoy: Identify common interests and make time for them. It could be hiking, cooking, or attending a workshop.
2. Start a New Tradition: Create annual rituals like a holiday gathering, a movie night, or a book club with your friends or family.
3. Be Spontaneous: Sometimes, unplanned moments like a surprise picnic or an impromptu road trip can be the most memorable.

Example: Two friends who commit to running a marathon together not only achieve a fitness goal but also strengthen their bond through shared training sessions.

4. Master the Art of Listening

Listening is the foundation of meaningful communication. It's not just about hearing words but about understanding emotions, intentions, and needs.

1. Why This Matters:

1. Active listening makes people feel valued and respected.
2. It helps you avoid misunderstandings and resolve conflicts more effectively.

2. How to Apply This Strategy:

1. Be Fully Present: Put away your phone or other distractions and give the person your undivided attention.
2. Use Reflective Responses: Paraphrase what the other person has said to confirm understanding. For example, "It sounds like you're feeling overwhelmed at work."
3. Ask Open-Ended Questions: Encourage deeper conversations by asking questions like, "What's been on your mind lately?"

Example: A partner who listens attentively to their significant other's concerns about work without interrupting builds trust and emotional intimacy.

5. Handle Conflicts with Care

Conflict is inevitable in any relationship, but how you handle it can either strengthen or weaken your bond. Approaching disagreements with empathy and respect is key.

1. Why This Matters:

1. Poorly handled conflicts can create resentment and distance, while skillful resolution fosters understanding and growth.
2. Respectful conflict management shows that you value the relationship over being "right."

2. How to Apply This Strategy:

1. Stay Calm: Take deep breaths and approach the conversation with a composed demeanour.
2. Focus on the Issue, Not the Person: Avoid personal attacks and concentrate on resolving the problem.
3. Seek Win-Win Solutions: Collaborate to find outcomes that meet both parties' needs.

Example: Two roommates arguing over chores can find a resolution by creating a clear and fair cleaning schedule that satisfies both.

6. Celebrate Milestones and Small Wins.

Acknowledging achievements, anniversaries, and even minor victories reinforces positivity in relationships.

- **Why This Matters:**
  - Celebrating together creates moments of joy and strengthens emotional bonds.

- o It shows that you value and notice the other person's accomplishments.

- **How to Apply This Strategy:**

  - o Make It Personal: Tailor celebrations to the person's preferences. For example, a book lover might appreciate a literary-themed gift.
  - o Don't Wait for Big Moments: Celebrate small wins like completing a project or overcoming a challenge.
  - o Express Genuine Excitement: Let your enthusiasm for their success shine through.

Example: A manager who publicly recognises an employee's effort on a project builds a stronger, more motivated team.

7. Show Gratitude Regularly

Gratitude is a simple yet powerful way to strengthen relationships. Expressing appreciation fosters mutual respect and affection.

- **Why This Matters:**

  - o Gratitude creates a positive feedback loop, encouraging both parties to invest more in the relationship.
  - o It counters negativity and helps repair strained connections.

- **How to Apply This Strategy:**

  - o Say Thank You: Verbally acknowledge acts of kindness or support.

- o Write a Gratitude Note: A handwritten letter or a thoughtful text can leave a lasting impression.
- o Publicly Recognise Contributions: In a professional setting, praise someone's efforts in front of others.

Example: A child who thanks their parent for always being supportive can deepen their bond through simple words of appreciation.

Bringing It All Together

Building meaningful relationships is a lifelong journey that requires consistent effort, empathy, and self-awareness. By prioritising quality over quantity, showing up consistently, investing in shared experiences, mastering listening, resolving conflicts gracefully, celebrating milestones, and expressing gratitude, you can create connections that stand the test of time.

Navigating Challenges in Relationships

1. Setting Boundaries

Healthy relationships require clear boundaries to protect your emotional well-being.

2. Letting Go of Toxic Connections

Not all relationships are meant to last. Learn to recognise when it's time to move on.

Exercises After Chapter 6

Exercise 1: Relationship Audit

Evaluate your current relationships—which ones bring joy and which ones drain you? Focus your energy on the connections that truly matter.

Exercise 2: The Gratitude Letter

Write a heartfelt letter to someone who has positively impacted your life. Share it with them to strengthen your bond.

Conclusion: Relationships Are Life's Greatest Treasure

At the end of the day, our relationships define the quality of our lives. They provide love, support, and purpose, reminding us that we're not alone. By investing time, effort, and care, you can build connections that enrich every aspect of your journey.

Quote: "In the end, what matters most is how well you loved, how well you lived, and how well you let go." – Anonymous

Now, take the first step. Reach out, reconnect, and nurture the relationships that matter most.

CHAPTER 7

Building Communication Skills

The Art of Expressing, Understanding, and Connecting

Why This Chapter Matters

Communication is the cornerstone of every meaningful relationship, personal or professional. It's how we express ourselves, understand others, and bridge the gaps that divide us. Yet, for many, communication is a source of frustration—misunderstandings, unresolved conflicts, or difficulty articulating thoughts.

This chapter explores how to master the art of communication. By the end, you'll have the tools to express yourself clearly, listen empathetically, and connect deeply with others. Whether you're navigating a tough conversation, giving a presentation, or strengthening personal relationships, these skills will transform the way you interact with the world.

Quote: "The single biggest problem in communication is the illusion that it has taken place." – George Bernard Shaw

What is Effective Communication?

Effective communication is the ability to convey information in a way that is easily understood and well-received while also understanding and valuing the other person's perspective. It goes beyond just speaking; it's about listening, nonverbal cues, and emotional intelligence.

The Pillars of Effective Communication

1. **Clarity:** Ensuring that your message is simple, direct, and easy to understand.
2. **Empathy:** Understanding the emotions and experiences behind someone else's words.
3. **Active Listening:** Fully engaging with what the other person is saying, not just hearing but processing and responding thoughtfully.
4. **Adaptability:** Tailoring your communication style to fit the audience or situation.

The Role of Communication in Success and Relationships

Professional Success

Good communication can open doors in your career. It builds trust with colleagues, strengthens leadership skills, and ensures you can present your ideas effectively.

Example: Think about the best leaders you've encountered. Chances are, they were exceptional communicators who inspired and motivated others.

Personal Fulfilment

Strong communication fosters understanding, reduces conflicts, and builds deeper relationships. It's what turns acquaintances into close friends and keeps relationships strong over time.

Quote: "Communication in a relationship is like oxygen to life. Without it, it dies." – Tony Gaskins.

The Science Behind Communication: A Deeper Dive

Communication is much more than the words we speak. It is deeply rooted in our biology and psychology, influencing how we connect, build relationships, and navigate the world. Let's explore three key scientific principles that shed light on how communication works and how you can master it.

1. The Role of Nonverbal Communication

Did you know that a majority of communication happens without words? Nonverbal cues—like facial expressions, tone of voice, and body language—play a significant role in how messages are delivered and received. Studies suggest that up to 93% of communication is nonverbal, meaning that what you say is often less important than how you say it.

Components of Nonverbal Communication:

- Facial Expressions: These are the most universally understood nonverbal signals. A smile, for instance, conveys warmth and friendliness, while a furrowed brow might indicate concern or confusion.

- Tone of Voice: The way you speak (pitch, speed, volume) adds emotional context to your words. For example, a calm tone can soothe, while a sharp tone might escalate tension.
- Body Language: Your posture, gestures, and physical movements reveal your confidence, openness, or discomfort. Crossing your arms might signal defensiveness, while leaning in can show interest.

Why Nonverbal Communication Matters:

Nonverbal cues provide context and clarity to spoken words. When verbal and nonverbal messages align, your communication is seen as trustworthy and credible. However, when they conflict (e.g., saying "I'm fine" with a frown), it creates confusion and mistrust.

Practical Tips to Master Nonverbal Communication:

1. Maintain Open Posture:

   1. Stand or sit upright with your shoulders relaxed and arms uncrossed. This signals approachability and confidence.

2. Use Gestures Intentionally:

   1. Emphasise key points with hand gestures. For instance, a sweeping motion can convey growth or expansion, while pointing to specific items reinforces focus.

3. Align Tone and Words:

   1. Make sure your tone matches the emotion behind your words. For example, an enthusiastic tone should accompany words of excitement or praise.

4. Observe Others:

1. Pay attention to other people's nonverbal cues to understand their emotional state or level of engagement.

Example: In a professional setting, maintaining steady eye contact and a firm handshake communicates confidence and sincerity.

2. Mirror Neurons and Emotional Connection

Mirror neurons are specialised cells in our brains that fire both when we perform an action and when we observe someone else performing the same action. These neurons are the biological basis of empathy, allowing us to "mirror" others' emotions and actions, fostering connection.

How Mirror Neurons Work:

1. Emotional Contagion: When you see someone smile, your mirror neurons activate, making you more likely to smile back. This creates a positive feedback loop, strengthening bonds.
2. Understanding Intentions: Mirror neurons help us intuitively grasp others' motives. For example, watching someone reach for a glass prompts your brain to anticipate their action.

Practical Applications for Communication:

1. Use Positive Body Language:

1. A smile or open posture can trigger similar responses in others, creating a welcoming atmosphere.

2. Pay Attention to Emotional Cues:

1.   Observe subtle changes in tone or facial expressions to better understand unspoken feelings.

3. Be Mindful of Negative Energy:

1.   If you project frustration or defensiveness, others may mirror it, escalating tension.

Example: Starting a meeting with a warm smile and an upbeat tone can set a positive tone, encouraging collaboration and open dialogue.

The Power of Small Gestures:

Even simple actions like nodding during a conversation or mirroring someone's body language can create a sense of rapport. It signals, "I understand you," fostering trust and connection.

3. The Psychology of Listening

Listening is often overlooked as a passive activity, but it's actually an active, brain-intensive process. When you listen, your brain's prefrontal cortex—responsible for focus, decision-making, and empathy—is hard at work, processing both spoken words and nonverbal cues.

What Active Listening Involves:

1.   Focusing Fully on the Speaker: Giving undivided attention ensures that you absorb the message without distractions.
2.   Processing and Reflecting: Paraphrasing what you've heard or asking clarifying questions shows that you are engaged.

3. Responding Thoughtfully: Thoughtful responses deepen understanding and build trust.

The Benefits of Active Listening:

1. Stronger Relationships: Listening creates a safe space for others to express themselves, strengthening bonds.
2. Better Problem-Solving: Fully understanding a situation allows you to address issues more effectively.
3. Improved Emotional Intelligence: Listening enhances your ability to empathise with others.

Practical Tips to Become a Better Listener:

1. Practice Mindfulness:

   1. Before engaging in a conversation, take a deep breath and clear your mind of distractions. Focus entirely on the present moment.

2. Avoid Interrupting:

   1. Resist the urge to jump in with your thoughts. Let the speaker finish their point before responding.

3. Paraphrase to Confirm Understanding:

   1. Summarise what the speaker has said to ensure you've understood correctly, e.g., "It sounds like you're feeling overwhelmed by the workload."

4. Use Nonverbal Listening Cues:

   1. Nod occasionally, maintain eye contact, and use encouraging expressions like smiling to show engagement.

Example: During a heated discussion with a colleague, instead of reacting defensively, an active listener might say, "I hear that you're frustrated about the timeline. Let's figure out how we can adjust it to make things manageable."

Transforming Conversations Through Listening:

Active listening is more than just a technique; it's a gift. By truly listening to someone, you show that you value and respect them, which can transform even strained relationships into constructive ones.

Bringing it Together

The science behind communication reveals that how we express and interpret messages is deeply rooted in our biology and psychology. By mastering nonverbal cues, leveraging the power of mirror neurons, and honing active listening skills, you can build deeper connections and navigate interactions with greater ease.

1. Nonverbal Communication: Focus on gestures, tone, and body language to align your words with your emotions.
2. Mirror Neurons: Harness empathy to foster rapport and understanding.
3. Active Listening: Stay present, process deeply, and respond thoughtfully to build trust.

When these elements come together, communication becomes more than an exchange of words—it becomes a powerful tool for connection, collaboration, and growth.

Case Studies: Real-Life Lessons in Communication

Case Study 1: Sarah's Career Breakthrough

Sarah, a talented graphic designer, often felt sidelined in team meetings. Her brilliant ideas were frequently overlooked because she struggled to articulate them clearly and confidently.

What She Did:

- **Joined a Toastmasters Club:**

  - Sarah practised public speaking in a supportive environment, which boosted her confidence.

- **Used Visual Aids:**

  - She started presenting her ideas with infographics and mock-ups, making them more engaging.

- **Learned to Summarise Effectively:**

  - Sarah adopted a structure: State the idea, explain the benefit, and invite feedback.

The Result:

Within months, Sarah's ideas became a cornerstone of team discussions. Her manager noticed her improved communication skills and promoted her to lead designer.

Key Takeaway: Combining clarity, confidence, and visual tools makes your ideas hard to ignore.

Case Study 2: Ravi's Family Conflict Resolution

Ravi's family dinners often ended in frustration. Conversations turned into heated debates, and unresolved tensions lingered for days. Realising the toll it was taking, Ravi decided to approach communication differently.

What He Did:

- **Facilitated Turn-Taking:**

  o Ravi suggested a rule: Each person speaks without interruption for two minutes.

- **Shifted the Focus to Emotions:**

  o He encouraged family members to share how situations made them feel, rather than just stating opinions.

- **Introduced Weekly Family Meetings:**

  o They used these sessions to discuss issues calmly and collaboratively.

The Result:

The family's conversations became more constructive, and conflicts were resolved more quickly. Ravi's new approach helped the family bond and improved their overall dynamics.

Key Takeaway: Structured communication can transform relationships by reducing misunderstandings and fostering empathy.

Case Study 3: Jay's Public Speaking Transformation

Jay, an introverted college student, dreaded public speaking. Despite being brimming with ideas, his fear held him back from leadership roles.

What He Did:

1. Joined a Debate Club:

1.   Jay pushed himself to practise in front of peers.

2. Prepared Thoroughly:

1.   He researched his topics extensively, giving him confidence in his knowledge.

3. Adopted Storytelling:

1.   Jay learned to hook his audience with relatable stories, making his speeches memorable.

The Result:

Jay's confidence grew exponentially, and he was elected president of his student organisation.

Key Takeaway: Public speaking is a skill that can be learned through preparation, practice, and perseverance.

Strategies for Building Communication Skills

1. Master Active Listening

Listening is the foundation of effective communication. It's about understanding, not just hearing.

1. Tips for Active Listening:

1. Maintain eye contact to show engagement.
2. Paraphrase what the other person has said to confirm understanding.
3. Avoid interrupting or planning your response while they are speaking.

2. Practice Clarity and Brevity.

Avoid overloading your message with unnecessary details. Be clear and concise.

Example: Instead of saying, "I think maybe we should try something different because this isn't really working," say, "Let's brainstorm alternatives to improve this process."

3. Use Nonverbal Communication Effectively

Nonverbal cues can enhance or undermine your message.

1. Key Techniques:

1. Use open gestures to appear approachable.
2. Match your facial expressions to your emotions.
3. Maintain a confident posture.

4. Develop Emotional Intelligence.

Understanding your own emotions and those of others is crucial for effective communication.

1. How to Develop Emotional Intelligence:

1. Reflect on your emotions before responding.
2. Practice empathy by considering how others might feel.
3. Learn to manage stress during tense conversations.

Emotional intelligence is the foundation for critical skills.

5. Adapt Your Style to Your Audience

Tailor your communication to fit the needs and preferences of your audience.

1. **Example:** Use formal language in a business setting, but keep things casual when chatting with friends.

Fun Activity: Communication Charades

1. **Objective:** Practice nonverbal communication by playing charades with friends or family.

2. **Instructions:**

   1.

2. Write down different emotions (e.g. happiness, frustration) or phrases (e.g. "I need help").
3. Act them out without speaking and have others guess.
4. Reflect on how body language and facial expressions convey meaning.

Exercises After Chapter 7

Exercise 1: Active Listening Challenge

Choose one person to focus on each day for a week. During conversations, practice:

1. Maintaining eye contact.
2. Paraphrasing their points.
3. Asking thoughtful follow-up questions.

Reflect on how this deepens your understanding and connection.

Exercise 2: Improve a Presentation

Pick a topic you're passionate about and prepare a short presentation. Focus on:

1. Clear and concise messaging.
2. Using gestures and visuals effectively.
3. Practising until you feel confident.

Deliver it to a friend or family member and ask for feedback.

Exercise 3: Nonverbal Experiment

Spend a day paying attention to your body language during interactions. Note moments where:

- Your posture was open or closed.
- Your tone matched your words.
- Your gestures enhanced your communication.

Write down observations and areas for improvement.

Conclusion: Communication is the Gateway to Connection.

Communication is more than just talking; it's about understanding, expressing, and connecting. Mastering active listening, clarity, nonverbal communication, and emotional intelligence will unlock the potential for deeper relationships, greater success, and a more fulfilling life.

Quote: "Good communication is the bridge between confusion and clarity." – Nat Turner

CHAPTER 8

Overcoming Procrastination

The Art of Taking Action and Staying Focused

Why This Chapter Matters

Procrastination is a universal struggle. At some point, everyone has delayed an important task, often trading productivity for short-term comfort. While it might seem harmless, procrastination can lead to stress, missed opportunities, and diminished confidence over time.

This chapter is your guide to understanding why we procrastinate, how to break the cycle, and what tools and strategies can help you build momentum. By learning to overcome procrastination, you'll unlock a powerful skill: the ability to take consistent, purposeful action towards your goals.

Quote: "You don't have to be great to start, but you have to start to be great." – Zig Ziglar

What is Procrastination?

Procrastination is the habit of delaying tasks or decisions, even when you know it's in your best interest to act. It's not just about laziness; it's often tied to fear, perfectionism, or lack of clarity.

The Common Types of Procrastinators

1. **The Perfectionist:** Delays starting because they fear their work won't be flawless.
2. **The Avoider:** Puts off tasks to escape feelings of discomfort or anxiety.
3. **The Thrill-Seeker:** Waits until the last minute to feel the adrenaline rush of racing against the clock.
4. **The Overwhelmed:** Feels paralysed by the size or complexity of a task.

Understanding which type resonates with you is the first step towards overcoming procrastination.

The Science of Procrastination: A Deeper Dive

Procrastination isn't just about laziness or lack of willpower; it's a complex interplay of neurological processes, emotional responses, and psychological tendencies. Understanding the science behind procrastination can help you address its root causes and develop practical strategies to overcome it.

1. The Role of the Brain: A Tug-of-War Between Planning and Pleasure

At its core, procrastination is the result of a battle between two key areas of the brain:

1. The Prefrontal Cortex: This is the brain's decision-making and planning centre. It helps you set long-term goals, prioritise tasks, and resist immediate temptations.
2. The Amygdala: This emotional centre of the brain seeks instant gratification and avoids discomfort. When you feel overwhelmed or stressed, the amygdala often overrides the prefrontal cortex, leading to procrastination.

The Battle in Action:

1. When you face a challenging task, such as studying for an exam or preparing a work presentation, your amygdala perceives it as a threat (e.g., "This is stressful and unpleasant").
2. To avoid discomfort, your brain seeks out quick rewards, like checking social media or watching TV. These distractions offer an immediate sense of relief, reinforcing the procrastination habit.

How to Rebalance the Brain:

1. Chunk Tasks: Break large tasks into smaller, manageable pieces to make them less intimidating for the amygdala.
2. Reframe Challenges: Instead of thinking, "I have to finish this daunting report," say, "I'll start with the introduction, it's manageable and low-pressure."

Example: A student overwhelmed by a 10-page research paper might procrastinate because the task feels insurmountable. By starting with one paragraph, the brain perceives the task as achievable, reducing resistance.

2. The Dopamine Effect: Why Distractions Feel So Good

Procrastination is closely tied to the brain's reward system, which is driven by dopamine, a neurotransmitter responsible for pleasure and motivation.

How Dopamine Fuels Procrastination:

1. When you choose a fun distraction over a challenging task, your brain releases dopamine, providing a quick sense of satisfaction.
2. Over time, your brain associates distractions (like social media or binge-watching) with immediate rewards, reinforcing the habit.

The Problem:

Dopamine from distractions is short-lived, and once it wears off, the stress of the uncompleted task returns, often worse than before.

How to Hack the Dopamine System:

1. Gamify Your Work: Turn tasks into mini-games with small, achievable goals and rewards. For example, reward yourself with a 5-minute break after completing 25 minutes of focused work.
2. Create Positive Triggers: Associate tasks with enjoyable rituals. For instance, listen to your favourite playlist while working or treat yourself to a snack after completing a step.

Example: Sarah, who struggles to exercise, combines her workouts with watching her favourite TV series. The anticipation of entertainment makes her more likely to start and stick to her routine.

3. Time Perception and Procrastination: Why We Disconnect from Our Future Selves

Human brains often struggle to perceive the urgency of long-term consequences, which is a major factor in procrastination. This disconnect makes it difficult to prioritise future rewards over immediate pleasures.

Why This Happens:

1. When thinking about future tasks, your brain treats your "future self" as a stranger. Tasks with distant deadlines, like saving for retirement or completing a project due in two months, feel less urgent.
2. Meanwhile, immediate gratification (like watching a funny video) feels more tangible and rewarding, leading to procrastination.

The Psychological Mechanism:

This is known as temporal discounting, where people value immediate rewards more than future benefits. For instance, spending money on a luxury today feels more rewarding than saving it for a vacation six months from now.

How to Overcome This Disconnect:

1. Visualise Your Future Self: Picture yourself enjoying the benefits of completing the task. For example, imagine the relief and pride of finishing your work on time.
2. Shorten Deadlines: Break long-term goals into smaller, time-sensitive milestones to create a sense of urgency.
3. Use Commitment Devices: Set up external constraints, like scheduling a meeting to discuss progress or using apps that block distractions.

Example: A writer working on a novel sets weekly word count goals and schedules progress updates with a friend. This keeps the project feeling immediate and manageable.

Practical Implications of the Science

Understanding the science behind procrastination helps you reframe your approach to tasks. Instead of viewing procrastination as a personal flaw, recognise it as a natural response that can be managed with the right tools and strategies.

1. Leverage the Prefrontal Cortex: Plan and prioritise tasks while keeping them manageable to avoid triggering the amygdala's stress response.

2. Optimise Dopamine Rewards: Shift the brain's reward system towards productive habits by associating them with positive reinforcement.

3. Reconnect with Your Future Self: Visualise long-term benefits to make them feel as rewarding as immediate distractions.

By applying these scientific insights, you'll not only overcome procrastination but also build habits that lead to lasting productivity and success.

Case Studies: Real-Life Lessons in Overcoming Procrastination

Case Study 1: Anna's Student Life Transformation

Anna, a college sophomore, constantly found herself cramming for exams and submitting assignments at the last minute. The stress was overwhelming, and her grades were slipping.

What She Did:

- **Used the Two-Minute Rule:** Anna committed to starting tasks for just two minutes. This simple action helped her overcome the inertia of starting.
- **Created a Reward System:** She rewarded herself with 20 minutes of her favourite TV show after completing study sessions.
- **Broke Down Big Tasks:** Instead of writing a 10-page paper all at once, Anna divided it into smaller sections, tackling one each day.

The Result:

Anna's grades improved, and she felt more in control of her time. Her stress levels dropped significantly, and she discovered the joy of early completion.

Key Takeaway: Starting small and rewarding progress can break the cycle of procrastination.

Case Study 2: Mark's Career Productivity Hack

Mark, a marketing professional, struggled with procrastination at work. Emails piled up, and deadlines loomed, leaving him feeling overwhelmed.

What He Did:

- **Adopted Time Blocking:** Mark scheduled specific hours for focused work, limiting distractions during these periods.
- **Used Accountability Partners:** He began sharing weekly goals with a colleague, who checked in on his progress.
- **Eliminated Temptations:** Mark silenced notifications and worked in a distraction-free environment.

The Result:

Mark's productivity soared, earning him praise from his manager. The structured approach helped him stay on top of tasks and regain confidence in his abilities.

Key Takeaway: Structuring your time and removing distractions can drastically improve focus and productivity.

Case Study 3: Sarah's Fitness Comeback

Sarah had been postponing her fitness journey for years, always saying, "I'll start next week." She felt unmotivated and unsure where to begin.

What She Did:

1. **Set Micro-Goals:** Sarah started with a five-minute daily workout instead of aiming for an hour-long gym session.
2. **Found an Accountability Partner:** She partnered with a friend who checked in daily to ensure she stayed consistent.
3. **Visualised Success:** Sarah placed a vision board with her fitness goals and motivational quotes where she could see them daily.

The Result:

Within months, Sarah built a sustainable fitness routine. Her small, consistent efforts snowballed into significant progress, boosting her energy and confidence.

Key Takeaway: Small, actionable steps can help you overcome the fear of starting and build lasting habits.

Strategies for Overcoming Procrastination

1. Start Small: The Two-Minute Rule

Commit to working on a task for just two minutes. Often, this small action is enough to overcome the inertia of starting.

Example: If you're avoiding writing an essay, spend two minutes brainstorming ideas. You'll likely find it easier to keep going once you start.

2. Break Tasks into Smaller Steps

Overwhelming tasks often lead to procrastination. Breaking them into smaller, manageable chunks makes them less intimidating.

Example: Instead of cleaning your entire house, focus on organising one drawer at a time.

3. Use Time Blocking

Dedicate specific time slots to tasks and stick to them. This creates a sense of urgency and reduces decision fatigue.

4. Eliminate Distractions

Identify and remove distractions that tempt you away from your work. This could mean silencing your phone, closing unnecessary tabs, or working in a quiet space.

5. Visualise Your Future Self

Imagine the satisfaction of completing a task and how it will benefit your future self. Visualisation can make the rewards feel more immediate.

Example: Picture yourself confidently presenting a finished project rather than stressing over incomplete work.

6. Build Accountability

Share your goals with a friend, mentor, or accountability partner who can check in on your progress. Knowing someone else is tracking your efforts can motivate you to follow through.

7. Reward Progress

Celebrate small milestones to keep yourself motivated.

Example: Treat yourself to a favourite snack after completing a difficult task or finishing a focused work session.

Fun Activity: Procrastination-Busting Jar

1. **Objective:** Make tackling tasks fun and spontaneous.

2. **Instructions:**

   1. Write down small, manageable tasks on slips of paper (e.g., "Organise one shelf," "Write 100 words," "Do 10 push-ups").
   2. Place them in a jar.
   3. When you're feeling unmotivated, draw a task from the jar and commit to completing it.

Exercises After Chapter 8

Exercise 1: Create a Task Ladder

1. Pick a big task you've been avoiding.
2. Break it down into 5-10 smaller steps, starting with the easiest.
3. Commit to completing one step per day until the task is done.

Exercise 2: The Accountability Challenge

Pair up with a friend or colleague. Share your weekly goals and check in with each other daily. Discuss progress and encourage.

Exercise 3: Dopamine Detox

1. Spend one hour without distractions—no phone, TV, or unnecessary browsing.
2. Use this time to focus on a task or reflect on your goals.
3. Notice how much more focused and productive you feel afterwards.

Conclusion: Procrastination is a Habit You Can Break.

Procrastination isn't a reflection of your abilities; it's a habit rooted in fear, overwhelm, or distraction. By understanding its causes and applying these strategies, you can reclaim your time and take purposeful steps towards your goals.

Quote: "The best way to get something done is to begin." – Unknown

Now, it's time to take action. Start small, stay consistent, and watch how momentum transforms your life.

Part III

Overcoming Challenges

CHAPTER 9

Embracing Failure

Turning Setbacks into Stepping Stones

Why This Chapter Matters

Failure is often seen as something to avoid, a sign of inadequacy or defeat. However, failure is an inevitable and essential part of growth. Every successful person has faced setbacks, and what sets them apart is their ability to learn, adapt, and persevere.

This chapter explores the transformative power of failure. By embracing your mistakes and viewing them as learning opportunities, you can build resilience, refine your strategies, and ultimately achieve your goals.

Quote: "I have not failed. I've just found 10,000 ways that won't work." – Thomas Edison.

What is Failure?

Failure is not the opposite of success, it's part of the journey to success. It's the feedback you receive when things don't go as planned, offering valuable insights into what works and what doesn't.

Common Misconceptions About Failure

1. Failure Means You're Not Good Enough: False. It means you're trying something challenging and stepping out of your comfort zone.
2. Successful People Never Fail: False. Most successful individuals fail repeatedly before achieving their goals.
3. Failure is Permanent: False. Every setback is temporary if you're willing to learn and move forward.

The Science of Failure

1. The Growth Mindset

Psychologist Carol Dweck's research highlights the importance of a growth mindset—the belief that abilities and intelligence can be developed through effort and learning. People with a growth mindset view failure as an opportunity to improve, while those with a fixed mindset see it as a limitation.

Practical Tip: Reframe your internal dialogue. Instead of saying, "I can't do this," say, "I can't do this yet."

2. Neuroplasticity: The Brain Learns Through Mistakes

Neuroplasticity is the brain's ability to adapt and rewire based on experiences. Mistakes stimulate the brain to identify patterns, make corrections, and strengthen problem-solving pathways.

Practical Tip: Reflect on what went wrong and identify specific steps for improvement. Each failure strengthens your brain's ability to adapt.

3. Emotional Resilience and Stress Regulation

Failure often triggers stress, but experiencing and overcoming setbacks builds emotional resilience. Managing the stress response (fight, flight, or freeze) helps you stay calm and focused during challenges.

Practical Tip: Practice mindfulness or deep breathing exercises to regulate your emotions during setbacks.

Case Studies: Real-Life Lessons in Embracing Failure

Case Study 1: J.K. Rowling's Road to Harry Potter

Before becoming one of the world's most successful authors, J.K. Rowling faced numerous rejections. Struggling as a single mother, she was rejected by 12 publishers before Bloomsbury finally accepted her manuscript for "Harry Potter and the Philosopher's Stone."

How She Persevered:

1. Rowling believed in her story and refused to give up, despite repeated setbacks.
2. She used each rejection as an opportunity to refine her work.

Key Takeaway: Rejection doesn't define your worth – it's part of the process. Perseverance and belief in your vision can lead to extraordinary success.

Case Study 2: Elon Musk's Visionary Failures

Elon Musk, the founder of Tesla, SpaceX, and other groundbreaking companies, has faced countless failures. SpaceX's first three rocket launches failed, nearly bankrupting the company.

How He Embraced Failure:

1. Musk analysed each failure, identifying technical flaws and implementing solutions.
2. He viewed each setback as a necessary step towards innovation.

Key Takeaway: Bold visions often come with high risks and failures. Learning from these failures is key to achieving groundbreaking success.

Case Study 3: Oprah Winfrey's Career Setback

Oprah Winfrey was fired from her first television job as an anchor. Her producers told her she wasn't fit for television.

How She Transformed Failure:

1. Oprah used the experience to identify her strengths and shifted to hosting talk shows, where her empathetic storytelling skills shone.
2. This pivot led her to become one of the most influential media personalities in history.

Key Takeaway: Failure often redirects you towards paths better aligned with your strengths and purpose.

Strategies for Embracing Failure

1. Reframe Failure as Feedback

Failure provides valuable data. Instead of seeing it as a setback, view it as feedback that helps you adjust and improve.

Example: A failed presentation can reveal areas for improvement, such as public speaking skills or content structure.

2. Develop a Growth Mindset

Embrace challenges and persist through difficulties. Believe that your skills and intelligence can grow with effort.

Activity: After a setback, write down three things you learned and how you'll approach similar situations differently in the future.

3. Practice Self-Compassion.

Treat yourself with kindness after failure, as you would a friend. Avoid harsh self-criticism, which can demotivate and inhibit growth.

Example: Instead of saying, "I'm terrible at this," say, "This didn't go as planned, but I'm learning and improving."

4. Take Action Despite Fear

Fear of failure often paralyses people into inaction. Break this cycle by focusing on the first small step you can take towards your goal.

Example: If you're afraid of starting a business, begin by researching your market or creating a rough plan.

5. Celebrate Small Wins.

Recognise and celebrate progress, no matter how small. This builds confidence and reinforces positive behaviour.

6. Build a Failure-Resilient Environment

Surround yourself with supportive people who encourage growth and see failure as part of the journey.

Example: Join a mastermind group or a supportive community that shares lessons learned from setbacks.

Fun Activity: Failure Stories

1. Objective: Normalise failure and see its learning potential.

2. Instructions:

1.   Write down three failures you've experienced.
2.   For each failure, list what you learned and how it helped you grow.
3.   Share one story with a friend or family member to inspire them.

Exercises After Chapter 9

Exercise 1: Failure Inventory

1.   Write down three significant failures from your past.
2.   Reflect on each: What went wrong? What did you learn? How did you grow?

3. Identify one lesson you can apply to current challenges.

Exercise 2: Fear-Setting Exercise

- Identify a goal or action you've been avoiding due to fear of failure.
- List your worst-case scenario and what you could do to recover.
- Write down the potential benefits of taking action.

Exercise 3: Growth Journal

Keep a journal where you record daily or weekly setbacks, along with:

- What happened?
- What you learned.
- How you'll approach similar situations differently.

Conclusion: Failure is the Foundation of Success

Failure is not the end of the road; it's a crucial step in the journey to success. By embracing failure, you gain the insights and resilience needed to reach your goals.

Quote: "Success is not final, failure is not fatal: It is the courage to continue that counts." – Winston Churchill

CHAPTER 10

Overcoming Self-Doubt

Breaking Free from Impostor Syndrome and Building Unshakeable Confidence

Why This Chapter Matters

Self-doubt. is one of the most significant barriers to achieving your full potential. Whether it's second-guessing your abilities, feeling like a fraud, or believing that success is due to luck rather than skill, self-doubt can hold you back from opportunities and personal growth.

This chapter focuses on identifying and overcoming self-doubt, particularly **impostor syndrome**, a common phenomenon among high achievers. Through stories, strategies, and exercises, you'll learn to build self-confidence and trust in your abilities, empowering you to pursue your goals without hesitation.

Quote: "Doubt kills more dreams than failure ever will." – Suzy Kassem

What is Self-Doubt?

Self-doubt is the feeling of uncertainty about your abilities, achievements, or decisions. While occasional doubt is normal, chronic self-doubt can lead to indecision, procrastination, and missed opportunities.

The Many Faces of Self-Doubt

1. **Impostor Syndrome:** Feeling like a fraud, despite evidence of success.
2. **Fear of Failure:** Avoiding challenges due to a fear of making mistakes.
3. **Comparison Trap:** Measuring your worth against others, often to your detriment.

What is Impostor Syndrome?

Impostor syndrome is a psychological pattern where individuals doubt their achievements and fear being exposed as a fraud. Despite external evidence of success, those experiencing impostor syndrome attribute their accomplishments to luck, timing, or other external factors.

The Five Types of Impostor Syndrome:

1. **The Perfectionist:** Believes everything must be flawless and criticises minor mistakes.
2. **The Expert:** Feels unqualified unless they know everything, fearing they'll be exposed.
3. **The Soloist:** Prefers to work alone, fearing collaboration might reveal their "inadequacies."
4. **Natural Genius:** Feels like a fraud if they struggle to master something on the first attempt.
5. **The Superhero:** Overworks to compensate for perceived shortcomings, equating success with hard work.

Example: A newly promoted manager might feel they're "not ready" for leadership despite their track record of competence and achievements.

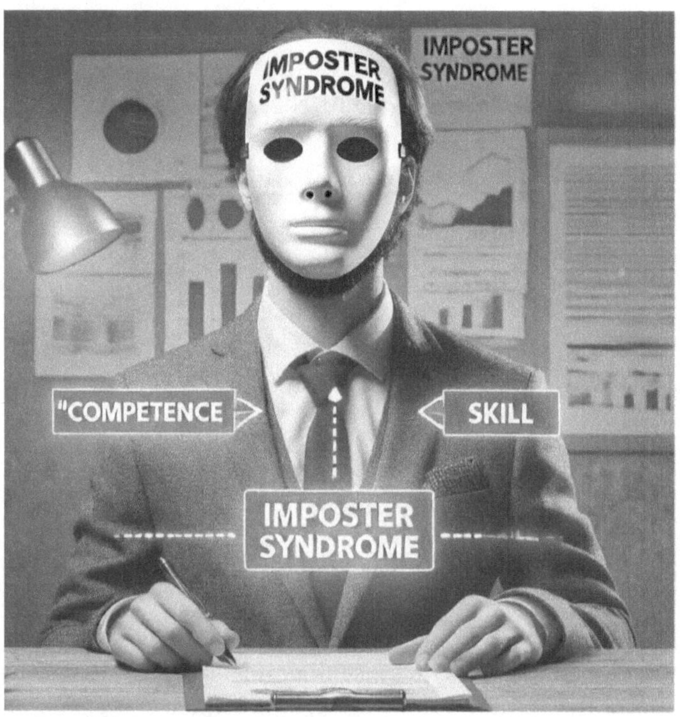

The Science of Self-Doubt

1. The Inner Critic: A Learned Voice

Self-doubt often stems from internalised criticism or societal expectations. The brain's **default mode network** (DMN), active during introspection, can amplify self-critical thoughts if left unchecked.

Practical Tip: Practice self-compassion by challenging negative self-talk with supportive, rational responses.

2. Confirmation Bias: Seeking Evidence to Validate Doubts

When plagued by self-doubt, the brain's **confirmation bias** searches for evidence that aligns with negative beliefs. For instance, a minor mistake might feel like proof that you're "not good enough."

Practical Tip: Keep a "success journal" to counterbalance negative bias with tangible achievements.

3. Neuroplasticity: Rewiring Confidence

The brain's ability to form new neural pathways (neuroplasticity) means that self-doubt isn't permanent. Repeatedly practising self-affirming behaviours can rewire your brain for confidence.

Practical Tip: Use visualisation exercises to rehearse success and reinforce positive beliefs.

Case Studies: Real-Life Lessons in Overcoming Self-Doubt

Case Study 1: Maya's Impostor Syndrome in Tech

Maya, a software engineer, felt unworthy of her role despite consistently delivering exceptional results. She often attributed her achievements to luck or help from colleagues.

How She Overcame It:

1. **Acknowledged Her Feelings:** Maya realised that impostor syndrome was common, even among high achievers.
2. **Tracked Her Achievements:** She created a portfolio of her projects and feedback to remind herself of her skills.
3. **Sought Mentorship:** Maya shared her feelings with a mentor who validated her abilities and provided guidance.

Key Takeaway: Recognising your worth and seeking support are essential steps to combating impostor syndrome.

Case Study 2: John's Fear of Public Speaking

John, a marketing professional, avoided presenting in meetings due to self-doubt about his communication skills.

How He Overcame It:

1. **Practised in Low-Stakes Settings:** John started by speaking in smaller groups to build confidence.
2. **Reframed Nervousness:** He saw it as a sign of caring about the outcome rather than as a weakness.
3. **Focused on Growth:** Instead of striving for perfection, John aimed to improve with each presentation.

Key Takeaway: Confidence is built through gradual exposure, reframing fears, and focusing on progress.

Case Study 3: Lisa's Battle with Perfectionism

Lisa, an artist, delayed launching her online store because she felt her work wasn't "good enough."

How She Overcame It:

1. **Set Deadlines:** Lisa committed to a launch date, forcing her to let go of perfectionism.
2. **Embraced Imperfection:** She reminded herself that growth comes from starting, not from waiting for perfection.
3. **Celebrated Small Wins:** Each step, from uploading photos to receiving her first order, reinforced her confidence.

Key Takeaway: Taking imperfect action is better than waiting for the "perfect" moment.

Elaborated Strategies for Overcoming Self-Doubt

1. Challenge Negative Thoughts.

Self-doubt thrives on irrational and self-critical beliefs that often have little basis in reality. Challenging these thoughts requires you to identify them, question their validity, and replace them with positive, rational alternatives.

How to Challenge Negative Thoughts:

1. Recognise the Thought:

1. Pay attention to your inner dialogue. Write down negative thoughts as soon as they arise.
2. Example: "I'm not smart enough to handle this project."

2. Question Its Validity:

1. Ask yourself:
    1. "Is there any evidence supporting this thought?"
    2. "Have I succeeded in similar tasks before?"
    3. "What would I tell a friend in my position?"
2. Often, you'll find that the thought is exaggerated or unfounded.

3. Replace It with a Rational Statement:

1. Turn the negative thought into a constructive one.
2. Example: Replace "I'm not smart enough to handle this project" with "I have the skills and determination to figure this out."

Practical Tip:

Keep a "Thought Reframe Journal" where you track negative thoughts, write down evidence for and against them, and replace them with positive affirmations.

2. Reframe Failure

Self-doubt often magnifies the fear of failure, making it seem catastrophic. Reframing failure as a natural and valuable part of learning helps you see it as an opportunity for growth rather than a reflection of your worth.

How to Reframe Failure:

1. Focus on the Lessons:

1. After a setback, reflect on what you learned and how it can help you improve.

2. Example: If you didn't get a job you interviewed for, identify areas for improvement (e.g. communication skills) and work on them.

2. Separate Effort from Outcome:

1. Acknowledge the effort you put into a task, even if the outcome wasn't what you wanted.
2. Example: "I prepared thoroughly for this presentation, and that's something to be proud of, regardless of how it was received."

3. Practice Self-Forgiveness:

1. Let go of self-blame and remind yourself that everyone makes mistakes.

Practical Tip:

Create a "Failure Inventory." List three past failures, write down what you learned from each, and note how those lessons helped you grow.

3. Build a Confidence Ritual

Confidence rituals are habits or routines that help you feel prepared and empowered before tackling a challenge. These rituals can ground you, reduce anxiety, and reinforce your belief in your abilities.

How to Build a Confidence Ritual:

1. Use Power Poses:

1. Stand tall, place your hands on your hips or raise them overhead for two minutes. Studies show that

power poses can increase feelings of confidence by reducing cortisol and boosting testosterone levels.

2. Create a Pre-Task Playlist:

1. Listen to uplifting music that energises you. Choose songs that make you feel unstoppable.

3. Visualise Success:

1. Close your eyes and picture yourself succeeding. Imagine the details—how you'll feel, what you'll see, and the reaction of others.

4. Speak Affirmations:

1. Repeat empowering statements like:
    1. "I am capable and prepared for this challenge."
    2. "I have handled challenges before, and I will handle this one too."

Practical Tip:

Develop a personalised "Confidence Kit" with items that boost your mood and motivation, such as a favourite book, a list of affirmations, or a success journal.

4. Seek Feedback and Support

Impostor syndrome and self-doubt often thrive in isolation. Seeking feedback and support from trusted individuals can help you see yourself through their eyes, providing a more accurate and balanced perspective.

How to Seek Feedback and Support:

1. Find a Mentor:

   1. A mentor can offer constructive feedback, share their experiences with self-doubt, and remind you of your strengths.

2. Ask for Specific Feedback:

   2. Instead of vague questions like "Do you think I'm good enough?" ask, "What are some ways I can improve in this area?"

3. Join Supportive Communities:

   3. Surround yourself with like-minded people who share their struggles and victories. Communities like professional networks, hobby groups, or masterminds can provide encouragement and validation.

4. Share Your Fears:

   4. Talking openly about your self-doubt can help normalise it. You might discover that even the people you admire face similar challenges.

Practical Tip:

Schedule regular check-ins with a mentor, coach, or accountability partner to reflect on your progress and gain insights.

5. Practice Self-Compassion.

Many people with self-doubt are harsh critics of themselves. Practising self-compassion involves treating yourself with kindness, recognising that imperfection is part of being human, and embracing moments of vulnerability as opportunities for growth.

How to Practice Self-Compassion:

1. Talk to Yourself Like a Friend:

    1. Imagine a close friend is experiencing your doubts. How would you comfort and encourage them? Offer yourself the same kindness.

2. Acknowledge Common Humanity:

    2. Remind yourself that everyone faces self-doubt and setbacks. You're not alone in your struggles.

3. Use Self-Soothing Techniques:

    3. Take a warm bath, practice deep breathing, or write a letter of encouragement to yourself.

Practical Tip:

Create a "Self-Compassion Script" with phrases like:

    1. "It's okay to feel this way. I'm doing the best I can."
    2. "I've overcome challenges before, and I'll get through this too."

How These Strategies Work Together

    1. Challenge Negative Thoughts helps you address the root of self-doubt.

2. Reframe Failure allows you to see setbacks as opportunities for growth.
3. Confidence Rituals empower you to face challenges with a positive mindset.
4. Feedback and Support provide external validation and guidance.
5. Self-compassion fosters resilience and emotional well-being.

By integrating these strategies into your daily life, you can dismantle the grip of self-doubt and build the confidence needed to pursue your goals.

Exercises for Boosting Self-Confidence

Exercise 1: Success Journal

1. Write down three achievements or proud moments each day.
2. Review this list regularly to remind yourself of your capabilities.

Exercise 2: Impostor Syndrome Reframe

1. Identify a self-doubt thought you've had recently.
2. Write down evidence that disproves this thought.
3. Replace it with a rational, empowering statement.

Exercise 3: Visualisation Practice

1. Spend 5 minutes daily visualising yourself succeeding in a specific task or goal.
2. Imagine the sights, sounds, and feelings associated with your success.

Exercise 4: Confidence Affirmations

1. Create a list of affirmations like:

    1.   "I am capable of achieving great things."
    2.   "I belong in this role because I've earned it."
    3.   "I learn and grow with every experience."

2. Repeat these affirmations each morning or before challenging situations.

Conclusion: Believe in Your Worth

Overcoming self-doubt is not about eliminating uncertainty – it's about acting despite it. By challenging negative thoughts, building self-compassion, and celebrating your achievements, you can quiet your inner critic and step confidently into your potential.

Quote: "You are braver than you believe, stronger than you seem, and smarter than you think." – A.A. Milne

Now, take the first step towards self-belief. Trust in your abilities and embrace your worth.

CHAPTER 11

Managing Stress and Mental Health

Balancing Life's Challenges with Emotional Resilience

Why This Chapter Matters

Stress is an inevitable part of life. While it can sometimes motivate us to take action, chronic stress harms our mental and physical health, impeding our ability to focus, perform, and enjoy life. Managing stress effectively isn't about eliminating it—it's about learning to navigate it with tools and strategies that promote resilience and well-being.

This chapter explores evidence-based techniques like mindfulness, therapy, and exercise to help you handle stress and maintain your mental health. By understanding the science of stress and implementing these strategies, you can achieve a healthier, more balanced life.

Quote: "It's not stress that kills us, it's our reaction to it." – Hans Selye.

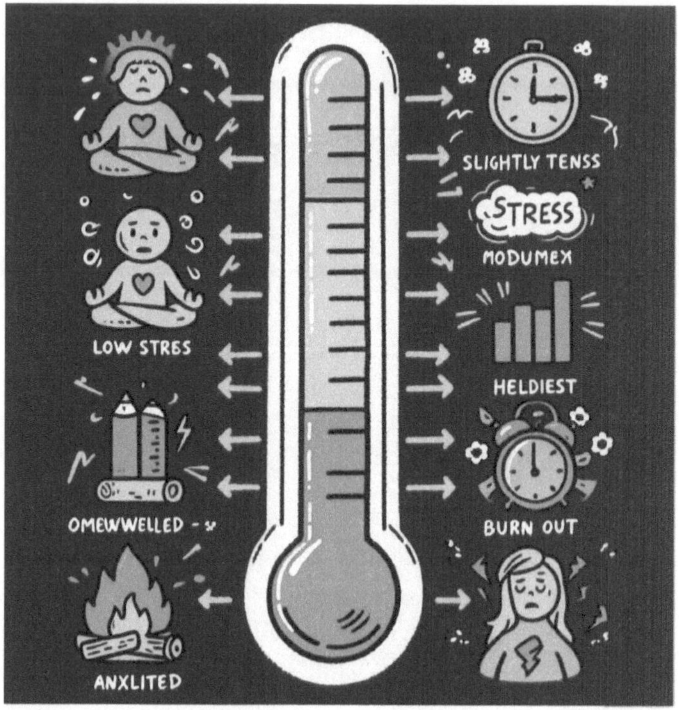

The Science of Stress

Stress is your body's response to any demand or challenge. This response involves physiological, psychological, and behavioural changes designed to help you cope. However, prolonged or excessive stress can lead to burnout, anxiety, and physical illness.

1. The Physiology of Stress

When you encounter a stressor, your body activates the **fight-or-flight response** through the hypothalamic-pituitary-adrenal (HPA) axis. This triggers the release of:

1. **Adrenaline:** Increases heart rate, sharpens focus, and boosts energy.
2. **Cortisol:** Mobilises energy by increasing glucose in the bloodstream but can impair health if elevated for too long.

Effects of Chronic Stress on the Body:

1. **Brain:** Impairs memory, learning, and emotional regulation due to prolonged exposure to cortisol.
2. **Heart:** Increases the risk of hypertension, heart disease, and stroke.
3. **Immune System:** Suppresses immune function, making you more susceptible to illness.

Practical Tip: Recognise stress signals such as tension headaches, fatigue, or irritability. These signals are your body's way of saying it's time to intervene with relaxation techniques.

2. The Role of Perception in Stress

Stress isn't solely about external events – it's influenced by how you perceive those events.

1. **Threat Mindset:** Interpreting situations as dangerous or overwhelming amplifies stress.
2. **Challenge Mindset:** Viewing stressors as opportunities to grow or learn mitigates their negative impact.

Reframing Stress:

- Replace "I can't handle this" with "This is a chance to develop new skills."
- Practice gratitude by identifying one positive aspect of a challenging situation.

Example: A manager preparing for a high-stakes presentation can reframe their anxiety as excitement, focusing on the opportunity to showcase their expertise.

3. The Nervous System and Stress Regulation

The autonomic nervous system governs the body's response to stress:

1. **Sympathetic Nervous System (SNS):** Activates during stress, preparing the body for action.
2. **Parasympathetic Nervous System (PNS):** Promotes relaxation and recovery, helping to restore balance.

Activating the PNS:

Techniques such as deep breathing, meditation, and progressive muscle relaxation can engage the PNS, calming the body and reducing stress levels.

Strategies for Managing Stress and Mental Health

1. Mindfulness: Cultivating Present-Moment Awareness

Mindfulness is the practice of bringing your full attention to the present moment without judgment. It is a powerful tool for reducing stress because it interrupts the cycle of negative thinking that often fuels anxiety.

How Mindfulness Works:

When stressed, your mind tends to fixate on past mistakes or future worries. Mindfulness shifts your focus to the here and now, activating the parasympathetic nervous system (PNS) to counteract the stress response.

Practical Mindfulness Techniques:

1. Mindful Breathing:

1. Sit or lie in a comfortable position. Close your eyes and focus on your breath.
2. Count your breaths: Inhale for 4 seconds, hold for 4 seconds, and exhale for 6 seconds.
3. Benefits: Calms the nervous system and lowers cortisol levels.

2. Body Scan Meditation:

1. Lie down and mentally scan your body from head to toe, noting any tension or discomfort.
2. Gently release tension as you focus on each area.
3. Benefits: Promotes relaxation and increases body awareness.

3. Mindful Walking:

1. Walk slowly, paying attention to each step and the sensations in your feet, legs, and body.
2. Engage your senses by noticing the sights, sounds, and smells around you.
3. Benefits: Combines physical activity with mindfulness for dual stress relief.

Example: Before a stressful meeting, practising mindful breathing for just five minutes can help calm your mind and allow you to approach the situation with clarity.

2. Therapy: Building Emotional Resilience

Therapy provides a safe and structured environment to explore your emotions, identify stressors, and develop coping strategies. It's particularly beneficial for addressing chronic stress, anxiety, and burnout.

Types of Therapy for Stress Management:

1. Cognitive-Behavioural Therapy (CBT):

   1. Helps you identify and reframe negative thought patterns that contribute to stress.
   2. Example: Replacing "I can't handle this workload" with "I'll focus on one task at a time to make progress."

2. Acceptance and Commitment Therapy (ACT):

   1. Encourages you to accept difficult emotions and commit to actions aligned with your values.
   2. Example: Recognising feelings of frustration but continuing to work on a meaningful project.

3. Talk Therapy:

   1. Provides a space to share your feelings, gain perspective, and receive emotional support.

Practical Tips for Therapy:

1. Find a therapist who specialises in stress management or your specific concerns.
2. Be consistent with sessions to build trust and track progress.

3. Combine therapy with self-care practices like journaling or relaxation techniques.

Example: Someone dealing with workplace stress might use CBT to challenge the belief that they must "do everything perfectly" and instead adopt a healthier mindset of prioritising key tasks.

3. Exercise: Movement as Medicine

Physical activity is one of the most effective ways to manage stress. Exercise reduces the body's stress hormones (like cortisol), releases mood-enhancing endorphins, and improves sleep quality.

How Exercise Helps Manage Stress:

1. Releases Endorphins: These "feel-good" chemicals improve mood and counteract anxiety.
2. Lowers Cortisol Levels: Physical activity helps metabolise excess stress hormones, reducing their negative effects.
3. Improves Sleep: Exercise promotes deeper, more restorative sleep, which is critical for stress recovery.

Types of Stress-Relieving Exercises:

- Yoga: Combines physical postures with breath control and meditation, promoting relaxation and flexibility.
- Running or Walking: Provides cardiovascular benefits and mental clarity through rhythmic movement.
- Strength Training: Builds physical strength while providing a healthy outlet for stress.
- Dancing: Combines aerobic activity with creativity and fun, boosting mood and energy.

Practical Tip:

Incorporate exercise into your daily routine by starting small—take a 10-minute walk or do a few stretches during breaks. Consistency is more important than intensity.

Example: A busy professional might start their morning with a 15-minute yoga session to centre themselves before a hectic day.

4. Social Connection: Leaning on Others

Humans are social beings, and strong relationships are a buffer against stress. Connecting with others provides emotional support, reduces feelings of isolation, and promotes a sense of belonging.

How Social Connection Reduces Stress:

1. Oxytocin Release: Positive social interactions trigger the release of oxytocin, a hormone that reduces stress and promotes feelings of well-being.
2. Shared Perspective: Talking through challenges with others helps you gain new insights and feel less alone.
3. Encouragement and Validation: Supportive relationships remind you of your strengths and capabilities.

Ways to Build Social Connection:

1. Spend time with friends and family who uplift and energise you.
2. Join groups or clubs that align with your interests or goals.

3. Volunteer for causes you're passionate about to meet like-minded people.

Example: Scheduling a weekly coffee date with a friend or attending a group fitness class can create opportunities for connection and stress relief.

5. Time Management: Reducing Overload

Poor time management often exacerbates stress, leading to feelings of overwhelm and burnout. Learning to prioritise tasks and set boundaries helps reduce mental and emotional strain.

Effective Time Management Techniques:

1. The Eisenhower Matrix:

1. Divide tasks into four categories: urgent/important, not urgent/important, urgent/not important, and neither. Focus on tasks in the first two categories.

2. Time Blocking:

1. Schedule specific blocks of time for work, rest, and leisure. This creates structure and ensures a balance between productivity and self-care.

3. Batch Processing:

1. Group similar tasks (e.g. responding to emails) and handle them all at once to minimise distractions.

4. Learn to Say No:

1. Protect your time by declining commitments that don't align with your priorities.

Practical Tip:

Set aside 15 minutes each evening to plan the next day, prioritising your top three tasks.

Example: A student juggling coursework and extracurriculars might use time blocking to dedicate focused study hours while ensuring time for relaxation.

6. Gratitude Practice: Shifting Focus to Positivity

Gratitude helps reframe your perspective by focusing on what's going well instead of dwelling on stressors. Studies show that practising gratitude can reduce stress, improve mood, and enhance overall well-being.

How to Practice Gratitude:

1. Daily Gratitude Journaling: Write down three things you're grateful for each day, no matter how small.
2. Gratitude Letters: Write a letter to someone who has made a positive impact on your life.
3. Gratitude Walks: Take a walk while reflecting on things you appreciate, such as nature, relationships, or personal achievements.

Example: Starting your day with a gratitude journal entry can help set a positive tone and build emotional resilience.

How These Strategies Work Together

Managing stress effectively requires a combination of strategies that address both the mind and body.

1. Mindfulness calms the mind and increases self-awareness.

2. Therapy provides tools to navigate complex emotions and stressors.
3. Exercise enhances physical health and emotional resilience.
4. Social Connection offers emotional support and encouragement.
5. Time Management reduces overwhelm by promoting structure and balance.
6. Gratitude Practice shifts focus from stressors to strengths, fostering positivity.

By integrating these strategies into your daily routine, you can create a holistic approach to stress management and mental health.

Fun Activity: Stress-Buster Jar

1. **Objective:** Create a personalised toolkit for stressful moments.

2. **Instructions:**

1. Write stress-relief ideas (e.g., "Take a 5-minute walk," "Call a friend," "Do 10 deep breaths") on slips of paper.
2. Place them in a jar.
3. When feeling stressed, draw a slip and complete the activity.

Exercises After Chapter 11

Exercise 1: Stress Log

1. Record stressors for a week, noting what triggered them and how you responded.

2. Reflect on patterns and identify stressors you can minimise or eliminate.

Exercise 2: Build a Relaxation Routine

1. Choose one relaxation technique (e.g., deep breathing, yoga) to practise daily.
2. Set aside 10–15 minutes each day for this activity.

Exercise 3: Gratitude Practice

1. Write down three things you're grateful for each day.
2. Reflect on how gratitude shifts your perspective and reduces stress.

Conclusion: Thriving Amid Stress

Stress is unavoidable, but how you respond to it determines its impact on your life. By incorporating mindfulness, seeking support, staying active, and prioritising self-care, you can transform stress into a catalyst for growth rather than a burden.

Quote: "You can't stop the waves, but you can learn to surf." – Jon Kabat-Zinn

CHAPTER 12

Leveraging Technology Wisely

Turning Digital Tools into Catalysts for Success

Why This Chapter Matters

This chapter focuses on how to use technology intentionally, turning it into a powerful ally rather than a distraction. Through practical strategies, examples, and inspiring stories, you'll learn to harness digital tools to enhance productivity, build connections, and achieve your goals.

Quote: "Technology is a useful servant but a dangerous master." – Christian Lous Lange

The Science of Technology and Behaviour

1. The Dopamine Loop of Digital Distraction

Social media and other digital platforms are designed to capture and hold your attention. Every like, notification, or message triggers the release of dopamine, the brain's "reward chemical," reinforcing the habit of checking your device repeatedly.

The Problem:

1. Excessive engagement with technology can lead to reduced focus, increased anxiety, and a fragmented attention span.
2. Multitasking between apps or devices lowers productivity by as much as 40% according to research.

Practical Tip:

Use apps like Focus Mode or digital well-being tools to limit notifications and track screen time.

2. The Power of Intentional Technology Use

When used intentionally, technology can amplify learning, streamline work, and foster meaningful connections. Studies show that integrating productivity apps and online learning platforms can increase efficiency and skill acquisition.

Strategies for Leveraging Technology Wisely

1. Social Media as a Tool vs. a Distraction

Social media can either be a powerful platform for networking and learning or a time sink that breeds comparison and distraction. The key is intentional use.

How to Use Social Media as a Tool:

1. Curate Your Feed:

1. Follow accounts that inspire, educate, or align with your goals (e.g. thought leaders, industry experts).

2. Unfollow or mute accounts that promote negativity or comparison.

2. Set Boundaries:

1. Allocate specific times for social media use, such as 15 minutes in the morning and evening.
2. Avoid mindless scrolling by setting a timer or using apps like StayFocusd.

3. Engage Purposefully:

1. Use social media to build relationships, share your work, and learn from others.
2. Example: A graphic designer might post portfolio samples on Instagram and connect with potential clients.

Example: Ali Abdaal, a popular productivity YouTuber, leverages social media to share insights, teach others, and grow his brand while limiting distractions through time management tools.

2. Productivity Tools for Organisation and Focus

Digital tools can help you stay organised, track goals, and manage your time effectively.

Must-Have Productivity Tools:

1. Task Management Apps:

1. Examples: Todoist, Trello, Notion.
2. Use these to create to-do lists, organise projects, and track deadlines.

2. Time Management Tools:

1. Examples: Forest, Focus@Will, or the Pomodoro Timer.
2. Block distractions and structure your work sessions for optimal focus.

3. Note-Taking Apps:

1. Examples: Evernote, OneNote, Obsidian.
2. Store ideas, research and notes in one place for easy access.

Example: A college student preparing for finals uses Notion to organise their study schedule, track progress, and store class notes in one seamless system.

3. Online Learning Platforms for Skill Development

The internet offers unparalleled access to knowledge and skill-building opportunities.

How to Leverage Online Learning:

1. Choose High-Quality Platforms:

1. Examples: Coursera, Udemy, Skillshare, Khan Academy.
2. Explore courses in your field or learn new hobbies to diversify your skills.

2. Set Clear Learning Goals:

1. Example: Commit to completing one course per month on a topic relevant to your career.

3. Engage Actively:

1. Take notes, apply what you learn, and participate in course discussions to deepen your understanding.

Example: An aspiring entrepreneur might use Udemy to learn digital marketing and SEO strategies and apply the knowledge to their online business.

4. Building an Online Personal Brand

A strong online presence can open doors to opportunities, whether you're a student, freelancer, or entrepreneur.

Steps to Build Your Brand:

- **Define Your Niche:**

  - **Focus on a specific area where you want to establish yourself as an expert (e.g., personal finance, graphic d**esign).

- **Create Valuable Content:**

  - Share tips, tutorials, or insights that resonate with your target audience.
  - Example: A fitness coach might post workout videos and nutrition advice on TikTok or YouTube.

- **Engage Authentically:**

  - Respond to comments, interact with followers, and participate in relevant online communities.

Example: Influencers like Marie Forleo and Gary Vaynerchuk built thriving businesses by leveraging their online presence to share knowledge and connect with audiences.

5. Setting Digital Boundaries for Balance

Technology should enhance your life, not control it. Setting boundaries ensures you use it productively while maintaining mental and emotional well-being.

How to Set Digital Boundaries:

1. Screen-Free Zones:

1. Designate areas in your home (e.g. bedroom, dining table) as technology-free spaces.

2. Digital Detox Days:

1. Commit to one day a week without social media or non-essential screen time.

3. Wind-Down Routine:

1. Turn off devices an hour before bedtime to improve sleep quality.

Practical Tip: Use apps like Moment or Digital Well-being to monitor and manage your screen time.

Example: A marketing professional might set a rule to avoid checking emails after 8 p.m. to preserve work-life balance.

Case Studies: Inspiring Uses of Technology

Case Study 1: Tim Ferriss's Life Optimisation

Tim Ferriss, author of *The 4-Hour Workweek*, uses technology to automate tasks, freeing time for creativity and learning.

1. **Tools He Uses:** Scheduling apps, autoresponders, and analytics tools to streamline work.
2. **Key Lesson:** Automating repetitive tasks with technology allows you to focus on high-impact activities.

Case Study 2: Zoe's Freelance Design Business

Zoe, a freelance graphic designer, built her career using digital tools:

1. **Portfolio Platform:** She showcased her work on Behance and Dribbble.
2. **Client Communication:** Zoe streamlined project updates using Slack and Asana.
3. **Online Learning:** She honed her skills with Photoshop tutorials on YouTube and Adobe's learning hub.

Result: Zoe attracted clients worldwide and scaled her business by leveraging technology purposefully.

Case Study 3: Marcus's Social Media Strategy

Marcus, a fitness coach, turned Instagram into a client magnet:

1. **Content Strategy:** He shared short workout videos and nutrition tips tailored to busy professionals.
2. **Engagement:** Marcus replied to comments and DMs to foster trust with followers.
3. **Collaboration:** He partnered with brands to promote fitness gear and supplements.

Result: Marcus grew his following to 100,000 and launched a successful coaching business.

Fun Activity: Your Digital Efficiency Audit

1. **Objective:** Identify how technology impacts your productivity and well-being.

2. **Instructions:**

   1. Track your screen time for one week using an app like Moment or Digital Well-being.
   2. Categorise usage: productive, recreational, or wasteful.
   3. Reflect on how to reduce distractions and optimise technology use for growth.

Exercises After Chapter 12

Exercise 1: Social Media Detox

   1. Take a 24-hour break from social media.
   2. Reflect on how it affects your mood, focus, and relationships.
   3. Implement one boundary to improve future use (e.g. no scrolling during meals).

Exercise 2: Build Your Digital Toolbox

   1. Identify one new tool (e.g. Notion, Asana) to enhance your productivity.
   2. Spend 30 minutes exploring its features and setting it up for daily use.

Exercise 3: Content Creation Challenge

   1. Choose a platform (e.g. Instagram, LinkedIn).
   2. Create and post one piece of content that shares your expertise or passion.
   3. Track engagement and reflect on how it aligns with your goals.

Part IV

Becoming Your Best Self

CHAPTER 13

Continuous Learning

The Power of Lifelong Growth and Adaptability

Why This Chapter Matters

In a rapidly changing world, the ability to learn continuously is no longer optional; it's essential. Lifelong learning equips you with the skills and knowledge to adapt to new challenges, stay relevant, and unlock opportunities. Whether it's mastering a new technology, developing a creative hobby, or advancing in your career, the commitment to growth is the foundation of personal and professional success.

This chapter delves into the importance of lifelong learning, introduces tools and platforms for expanding your skills, and highlights real-life examples of individuals who've transformed their lives through continuous education.

Quote: "Once you stop learning, you start dying." – Albert Einstein

The Science of Lifelong Learning

Lifelong learning is not just a philosophical concept; it is deeply rooted in neuroscience, psychology, and biology.

The ability to continuously acquire and apply knowledge depends on how the brain adapts and functions over time. Understanding the scientific mechanisms behind lifelong learning reveals why it's not only possible but also highly beneficial at any age.

1. Neuroplasticity: The Brain's Ability to Adapt

Neuroplasticity is the brain's ability to reorganise itself by forming new neural connections throughout life. This phenomenon allows the brain to adapt to new experiences, environments, and challenges, making learning and growth possible at any age.

How Neuroplasticity Works:

1. **Creating New Pathways:** When you learn a new skill, your brain forms connections between neurons, creating a pathway.
2. **Strengthening Pathways:** Repetition and practice reinforce these connections, making the skill or knowledge easier to recall and use.
3. **Pruning Unused Connections:** The brain eliminates weaker, unused pathways, optimising itself for efficiency.

Benefits of Neuroplasticity:

- **Improved Cognitive Abilities:** Learning enhances problem-solving, critical thinking, and memory.
- **Adaptability:** The brain's flexibility allows you to acquire new skills even as the world evolves.
- **Delay of Cognitive Decline:** Engaging in continuous learning reduces the risk of age-related mental decline, such as dementia.

Example: A middle-aged individual learning a musical instrument activates and strengthens neural pathways related to motor skills, auditory processing, and memory.

Practical Tip:

Engage in challenging and varied activities, such as learning a language or picking up a new hobby, to maximise neuroplasticity.

2. Dopamine and Motivation in Learning

Dopamine, the brain's "reward chemical", plays a critical role in learning and motivation. When you engage in a rewarding activity, your brain releases dopamine, reinforcing the behaviour and encouraging repetition.

How Dopamine Enhances Learning:

1. **Positive Feedback Loop:** Successfully learning or achieving something triggers dopamine release, motivating you to continue.
2. **Reward Prediction:** The brain anticipates rewards for effort, driving focus and perseverance.

The Challenge of Habits:

Modern distractions, such as social media, hijack the brain's dopamine system, making it harder to focus on meaningful learning.

Practical Tip:

Set small, achievable learning goals to create frequent dopamine rewards and maintain motivation. For example, celebrate milestones like completing a module in an online course.

3. The Role of the Hippocampus in Memory Formation

The **hippocampus**, a key part of the brain, plays a central role in forming and retrieving memories. It is especially active during learning as it organises information and integrates it with existing knowledge.

How the Hippocampus Supports Learning:

1. **Encoding Information:** The hippocampus transforms new information into long-term memory.
2. **Retrieving Knowledge:** It acts as a library, pulling relevant memories when needed.
3. **Spatial Learning:** Helps in navigating and understanding spatial environments (e.g., learning the layout of a new city).

Practical Tip:

Engage in spaced repetition, reviewing material over time to strengthen hippocampal encoding and retrieval. Apps like Anki can help.

Example: A language learner who reviews vocabulary daily builds stronger memory networks, allowing for faster recall in conversations.

4. Emotional Benefits of Learning

Learning isn't just good for the brain—it's also good for emotional health. Acquiring new skills and knowledge boosts confidence, self-esteem, and overall happiness.

Why Learning Improves Emotional Health:

1. **Sense of Achievement:** Mastering a new skill provides a sense of purpose and accomplishment.
2. **Increased Resilience:** Tackling challenges in learning builds resilience, helping you handle other life stressors.
3. **Social Connection:** Learning often involves collaboration, fostering relationships, and community.

Practical Tip:

Choose learning activities that align with your passions and interests to maximise emotional rewards.

5. Cognitive Reserve and Lifelong Learning

The concept of **cognitive reserve** refers to the brain's ability to compensate for age-related decline. Lifelong learning builds this reserve, enabling the brain to maintain functionality despite ageing or injury.

Building Cognitive Reserve:

1. **Engage in Diverse Activities:** Challenge your brain with a variety of learning experiences, such as reading, problem-solving, and creative pursuits.
2. **Stay Physically Active:** Exercise supports brain health by improving blood flow and stimulating the growth of new neurons.
3. **Foster Curiosity:** Cultivate a mindset of exploration and experimentation to keep your brain engaged.

Example: A retiree who learns to play chess and joins a local club strengthens their cognitive reserve while enjoying social interaction.

6. Learning Through Mistakes

Mistakes are an integral part of the learning process. When you make an error, your brain activates the **anterior cingulate cortex (ACC)**, which helps identify what went wrong and prompts adjustments.

Why Mistakes Enhance Learning:

1. **Error Correction:** The brain learns by identifying errors and exploring alternative approaches.
2. **Growth Through Challenge:** Struggling with a task strengthens problem-solving abilities and builds resilience.

Practical Tip:

Embrace failure as a teacher. Reflect on mistakes, adjust your approach, and try again.

Example: A student struggling with a math problem improves their understanding by analysing their errors and applying new strategies.

7. Social Learning and Mirror Neurons

Learning through observation activates **mirror neurons** in the brain, which mimic the actions or emotions of others. This mechanism allows you to learn by watching and interacting with others.

Benefits of Social Learning:

1. **Faster Skill Acquisition:** Observing experts can accelerate your learning process.

2. **Collaboration:** Sharing ideas and feedback enhances understanding.
3. **Emotional Connection:** Learning with others fosters empathy and motivation.

Practical Tip:

Join study groups, workshops, or mentorship programmes to enhance your learning experience through collaboration.

How These Scientific Principles Work Together

1. **Neuroplasticity** ensures your brain can adapt and grow, no matter your age.
2. **Dopamine** keeps you motivated and engaged.
3. **The hippocampus** helps store and retrieve knowledge, forming the foundation of memory.
4. **Cognitive reserve** and **social learning** enhance your ability to navigate challenges with resilience and creativity.

By understanding and leveraging these mechanisms, you can unlock the full potential of lifelong learning and apply it to personal and professional growth.

Strategies for Continuous Learning

1. Embrace a Growth Mindset.

The foundation of continuous learning lies in adopting a **growth mindset,** the belief that abilities and intelligence can be developed through effort, strategies, and support. This mindset helps you view challenges and setbacks as opportunities rather than failures.

Key Principles of a Growth Mindset:

1. **Effort Leads to Improvement:** Every skill starts with effort.
2. **Challenges Foster Growth:** The harder the task, the greater the opportunity for development.
3. **Feedback is Valuable:** Constructive criticism is a tool for improvement.

Practical Tips:

1. **Reframe Negative Thoughts:** Replace "I can't do this" with "I can learn to do this."
2. **Seek Feedback:** Actively ask for input on your work and use it to improve.
3. **Celebrate Progress:** Acknowledge milestones, even small ones, to reinforce effort and persistence.

Example: A professional who struggles with public speaking might take incremental steps like practising in front of a mirror, then with friends, before presenting to larger audiences.

2. Leverage Online Learning Platforms.

The internet provides unparalleled access to courses, tutorials, and resources. By tapping into online platforms, you can learn anytime, anywhere, at your own pace.

Popular Platforms:

- **Coursera and edX:** Offer university-level courses in fields like business, technology, and humanities.
- **Skillshare and Udemy:** Focus on practical skills such as graphic design, video editing, and writing.

- **YouTube:** Hosts countless free tutorials on virtually any topic.
- **Khan Academy:** Perfect for foundational learning in math, science, and more.
- **LinkedIn Learning:** Tailored for professionals looking to enhance workplace skills.

How to Maximise Online Learning:

1. **Set Clear Goals:** Know why you're taking the course and what you aim to achieve.
2. **Engage Actively:** Take notes, participate in discussions, and apply what you learn.
3. **Be Consistent:** Dedicate regular time slots for learning to build momentum.

Example: A graphic designer takes a Skillshare course on advanced Photoshop techniques to enhance their portfolio and attract higher-paying clients.

3. Read Widely and Deeply

Reading is one of the most accessible ways to expand your knowledge and perspective. Books, articles, and research papers expose you to new ideas, cultures, and skills.

How to Build a Reading Habit:

1. **Set a Daily Goal:** Commit to reading for at least 20 minutes a day.
2. **Diversify Your Reading:** Alternate between fiction, non-fiction, and professional resources.
3. **Use Technology:** Apps like Kindle, Audible, or Scribd make reading convenient and portable.

Recommended Genres for Lifelong Learners:

1. **Self-Improvement:** Books like *Atomic Habits* by James Clear.
2. **Biographies:** Learn from the lives of successful individuals like *Steve Jobs* by Walter Isaacson.
3. **Technical Skills:** Read industry-specific books to deepen your expertise.

Example: A teacher reads *Grit* by Angela Duckworth to better understand how to foster perseverance in their students.

4. Learn by Doing

Practical application is one of the most effective ways to retain and deepen knowledge. Actively engaging with what you've learned helps solidify concepts and identify gaps in understanding.

How to Apply What You Learn:

1. **Create Projects:** If you're learning to code, build a website. If you're studying photography, curate a photo series.
2. **Solve Real Problems:** Use new skills to address challenges at work or in your personal life.
3. **Teach Others:** Explaining concepts to others reinforces your understanding.

Example: An entrepreneur takes an online course on digital marketing and immediately applies the strategies to their business, running their first successful ad campaign.

5. Join Learning Communities

Learning is amplified when you're part of a supportive group. Communities provide motivation, accountability, and opportunities for collaboration.

Where to Find Learning Communities:

1. **Online Forums:** Platforms like Reddit and Quora host communities for almost every topic.
2. **Local Meetups:** Attend workshops or networking events in your area.
3. **Social Media Groups:** Join Facebook or LinkedIn groups aligned with your interests.
4. **Study Groups:** Partner with peers to share insights and tackle challenges together.

Benefits of Learning Communities:

1. Access to diverse perspectives and ideas.
2. Encouragement and accountability from peers.
3. Networking opportunities for personal and professional growth.

Example: A software developer joins a Reddit community for Python enthusiasts to share projects, ask questions, and stay updated on new trends.

6. Develop a Personalised Learning Plan

A learning plan helps you stay focused, track progress, and achieve your goals efficiently.

How to Create a Learning Plan:

1. **Identify Goals:** What skill or knowledge do you want to gain? Why?
2. **Break Down Steps:** Outline specific milestones or sub-skills to achieve your goal.
3. **Set a Timeline:** Allocate time for each step, keeping deadlines realistic yet challenging.
4. **Evaluate Progress:** Reflect regularly on what's working and adjust your plan as needed.

Example: A finance professional plans to earn a certification in data analysis within six months by dedicating 10 hours per week to online courses and practice projects.

7. Incorporate Gamification for Motivation

Gamification uses elements of game design—such as points, levels, and rewards—to make learning more engaging and enjoyable.

How to Gamify Your Learning:

1. **Set Challenges:** Create mini-goals like completing a module or mastering a specific skill.
2. **Reward Progress:** Treat yourself after achieving milestones (e.g., a favourite snack, break, or new gadget).
3. **Track Achievements:** Use apps like Habitica or Duolingo that turn learning into a game with levels and streaks.

Example: A language learner uses Duolingo to maintain a 100-day streak, feeling motivated by the progress tracking and achievement badges.

8. Stay Curious and Open-Minded

Cultivating curiosity leads you to ask questions, explore new topics, and maintain a lifelong love of learning.

How to Foster Curiosity:

1. **Ask Questions:** Approach every situation with a sense of wonder. Ask, "Why?" or "How?" to dive deeper.
2. **Try New Experiences:** Step out of your comfort zone to explore unfamiliar hobbies, cultures, or fields.
3. **Follow Your Passions:** Pursue topics that genuinely excite and energise you.

Example: A mechanical engineer develops an interest in 3D printing, exploring its applications beyond work, such as creating custom designs for fun.

How These Strategies Work Together

- **A Growth Mindset** provides the belief that you can improve and sets the foundation for lifelong learning.
- **Online Platforms and Communities** make resources and collaboration accessible.
- **Learning by Doing and Personalised Plans** ensure the knowledge gained is applied effectively.
- **Reading, Gamification, and Curiosity** keep the process engaging and sustainable.

By combining these strategies, you can create a lifelong learning routine that evolves with your goals and interests.

Case Studies on Continuous Learning

Case Study 1: Sarah's Career Pivot to Digital Marketing

Background:

Sarah, a 35-year-old marketing professional, found herself struggling as her company shifted towards digital platforms. She had a traditional marketing background and felt ill-equipped to compete in a market increasingly dominated by digital strategies like SEO, social media marketing, and analytics.

Challenge:

Sarah experienced self-doubt and feared she might become obsolete in her field. She wanted to stay relevant and advance her career, but felt overwhelmed by the amount of new information she needed to learn.

Actions Taken:

1. Set a Goal:

1. Sarah decided to master digital marketing within six months to improve her chances of landing a higher-paying, future-proof role.

2. Choose Online Learning Platforms:

1. She enrolled in Coursera's "Digital Marketing Specialisation," which provided structured courses covering SEO, analytics, and social media.

3. Practised on Real Projects:

1. Sarah volunteered to manage her friend's small business social media accounts, applying her new skills in a practical setting.

4. Built a Support System:

1. She joined a LinkedIn group for digital marketers, where she connected with professionals, asked questions, and received advice.

Results:

After six months, Sarah earned a certification in digital marketing and successfully transitioned into a role as a Digital Marketing Manager. Her salary increased by 30%, and she gained confidence in her ability to adapt to industry changes.

Key Takeaway:

Continuous learning enables career pivots and keeps you competitive in an evolving job market.

Case Study 2: John's Creative Hobby Transformed into a Side Hustle

Background:

John, a high school teacher, had always been interested in art but never pursued it seriously. During the COVID-19 lockdown, he found himself with extra time and a desire to learn something new.

Challenge:

John felt intimidated by the technical aspects of watercolour painting and doubted his ability to create professional-looking art. He needed an approachable way to start without feeling overwhelmed.

Actions Taken:

1. Started with Online Tutorials:

John began by watching free YouTube videos on watercolour basics, such as brush techniques and colour blending.

2. Took Structured Courses:

He later enrolled in Skillshare classes to deepen his understanding of advanced techniques like layering and perspective.

3. Practised Consistently:

John dedicated 30 minutes a day to painting, gradually improving his skills and experimenting with different styles.

4. Shared His Work:

He started posting his paintings on Instagram, where he received encouraging feedback from friends and strangers.

5. Monetised His Hobby:

As his confidence grew, John began accepting commissions for custom artwork and selling prints on Etsy.

Results:

John's side hustle now generates an extra $500–$700 per month, supplementing his teaching income. Beyond the financial benefits, painting became a source of relaxation and pride.

Key Takeaway:

A hobby pursued through continuous learning can evolve into a rewarding and profitable endeavour.

Case Study 3: Elena's Language Journey with Duolingo

Background:

Elena, a 62-year-old retiree, wanted to learn Spanish to communicate with her son-in-law's family and better connect with her bilingual grandchildren. Despite her enthusiasm, she felt intimidated by the idea of learning a new language at her age.

Challenge:

Elena doubted her ability to retain new information and feared she would embarrass herself by making mistakes when speaking.

Actions Taken:

1. Used a Gamified App:

Elena started learning Spanish with Duolingo, which broke lessons into bite-sized modules and made the process enjoyable with streaks and rewards.

2. Practised Speaking Daily:

She practised phrases with her grandchildren, who helped correct her pronunciation in a supportive way.

3. Joined a Language Exchange Group:

Elena participated in weekly online meetings where she practised conversational Spanish with native speakers in exchange for helping them practice English.

4. Immersed Herself in the Language:

She watched Spanish-language shows with subtitles and listened to beginner-level podcasts.

Results:

Within a year, Elena could hold basic conversations in Spanish, earning the admiration of her family and deepening her bond with her grandchildren. Learning Spanish also boosted her confidence, proving to herself that age is not a barrier to acquiring new skills.

Key Takeaway:

With the right tools and support, continuous learning can help overcome personal challenges and strengthen relationships.

Case Study 4: Tim Ferriss and Automated Learning for Optimisation

Background:

Tim Ferriss, author of *The 4-Hour Workweek*, is known for his focus on optimising productivity and learning.

He exemplifies the idea of learning efficiently to master diverse skills, from language acquisition to business automation.

Challenge:

Tim sought to achieve more with less effort by automating tasks and learning high-impact skills that improved his personal and professional life.

Actions Taken:

1. Applied the Pareto Principle:

He focused on the 20% of activities that yielded 80% of results. For example, he learned 1,000 core vocabulary words in multiple languages to achieve conversational fluency quickly.

2. Used Digital Tools:

1. For task automation: Set up autoresponders and scheduling tools to free up time for learning.
2. For language learning: Use apps like Anki for spaced repetition.

3. Experimented with Learning Hacks:

Tim used unconventional approaches, such as deconstructing skills into smaller, manageable parts, to learn them faster.

4. Sought Expert Guidance:

He interviewed specialists and mentors to gain insights and refine his strategies.

Results:

Tim's approach allowed him to build a highly successful personal brand, write best-selling books, and master various skills like cooking, martial arts, and podcasting—all while maintaining a balanced lifestyle.

Key Takeaway:

Efficiency in learning and automation can maximise productivity, leaving more time for personal growth and exploration.

Case Study 5: Lisa's Career Growth Through Self-Directed Learning

Background:

Lisa, a software developer, realised her skills in backend programming were becoming outdated as her company moved towards cloud computing and DevOps practices. She decided to upskill to stay competitive.

Challenge:

Lisa struggled to find time for learning alongside her demanding job and felt overwhelmed by the breadth of new technologies to master.

Actions Taken:

1. Identified Priorities:

Lisa researched and identified the most in-demand tools and certifications in cloud computing, focusing on AWS (Amazon Web Services).

2. Enrolled in Certification Programmes:

She completed an AWS certification course on A Cloud Guru, dedicating one hour a day to study.

3. Hands-On Practice:

Lisa built a small cloud-based application to apply her knowledge in a real-world context.

4. Sought Mentorship:

She connected with an experienced DevOps engineer who provided guidance and feedback.

Results:

Lisa earned her AWS certification and was promoted to a Cloud Solutions Architect role within her company, with a 25% salary increase.

Key Takeaway:

Focused, self-directed learning can help you adapt to industry changes and unlock career advancement.

How These Case Studies Inspire Action

1. **Career Shifts:** Sarah and Lisa show how learning new skills can open doors to better opportunities.
2. **Personal Growth:** John and Elena demonstrate that hobbies and personal goals can enrich your life and confidence.
3. **Efficient Learning:** Tim Ferriss exemplifies how to optimise learning for maximum impact.

Each case highlights the transformative power of continuous learning, proving that anyone can achieve personal and professional growth with the right mindset, tools, and strategies.

Exercises After Chapter 13

Exercise 1: Learning Goal Setting

1. Identify a skill or subject you've always wanted to learn.
2. Set a SMART (Specific, Measurable, Achievable, Relevant, Time-Bound) goal for learning it.
3. List one action you'll take this week to get started.

Exercise 2: Explore an Online Platform

1. Choose one online learning platform (e.g. Coursera, Skillshare).
2. Browse courses and select one to complete in the next month.

Exercise 3: Lifelong Learning Plan

1. Write down three areas of interest (e.g. career, hobbies, self-development).
2. For each, list one resource or activity to pursue.

Conclusion: Learning as a Lifelong Adventure

Lifelong learning is not just about staying competitive—it's about staying curious and fulfilled. By embracing a growth mindset, leveraging resources, and engaging with others, you can unlock endless opportunities for personal and professional growth.

Quote: "The beautiful thing about learning is that no one can take it away from you." – B.B. King

CHAPTER 14

Health and Fitness

Achieving Balance in Nutrition, Exercise, and Sleep

Why This Chapter Matters

Your physical health forms the foundation of your mental well-being, energy levels, and ability to achieve your goals. Neglecting it can lead to burnout, low productivity, and chronic stress. Achieving balance in **nutrition**, **exercise**, and **sleep** helps you maintain a fit body and a sharp, focused mind.

This chapter explores practical strategies for optimising these three pillars of health, empowering you to live your best life while working towards your ambitions.

Quote:"Take care of your body. It's the only place you have to live." – Jim Rohn.

The Science of Health and Fitness

Understanding the science behind health and fitness empowers you to make informed decisions about your body and mind. Each pillar—nutrition, exercise, and sleep—plays a distinct yet interconnected role in your overall well-being. Let's delve deeper into the scientific principles that underpin these essential components.

1. Nutrition: Fuel for Your Body and Brain

Nutrition provides the energy and nutrients your body needs to function efficiently. A balanced diet enhances not only physical performance but also cognitive function, mood, and long-term health.

Macronutrients: Building Blocks of Nutrition

- **Carbohydrates:**
  - Primary energy source for the body.
  - Complex carbs (like whole grains and vegetables) release energy slowly, providing sustained fuel. Simple carbs (like sugar) cause rapid spikes and crashes in energy.

- **Proteins:**
  - Essential for repairing and building tissues, especially muscles.
  - Composed of amino acids, which play a key role in hormone production and immune function.

- **Fats:**
  - Support brain health, hormone regulation, and energy storage.
  - Healthy fats (like omega-3s) reduce inflammation and improve cardiovascular health.

Micronutrients: The Small Yet Mighty Players

1. Vitamins:

1. Vital for metabolism, immune function, and preventing deficiencies. For example, vitamin D supports bone health and immunity.

2. Minerals:

1. Crucial for nerve function, hydration, and bone strength. For example, magnesium aids muscle relaxation and reduces stress.

The Brain-Nutrition Connection:

1. Foods rich in omega-3 fatty acids (found in fish, walnuts, and flaxseeds) enhance brain function.
2. Antioxidant-rich foods like berries combat oxidative stress, protecting brain cells from ageing.
3. A Mediterranean diet, which includes vegetables, lean proteins, and healthy fats, is linked to lower risks of depression and cognitive decline.

2. Exercise: The Science of Movement

Physical activity is more than just burning calories; it optimises nearly every system in your body, from the cardiovascular to the endocrine system.

Aerobic Exercise: Boosting Heart and Lung Health

1. How It Works: Aerobic exercises like running, swimming, and cycling increase your heart rate and improve oxygen flow throughout your body.

2. Benefits:

1. Enhances cardiovascular efficiency, reducing the risk of heart disease.
2. Stimulates the production of brain-derived neurotrophic factor (BDNF), which supports brain cell growth and memory.
3. Increases endorphins, improving mood and reducing stress.

Strength Training: Building Muscle and Metabolism

1. How It Works: Lifting weights or performing resistance exercises creates microtears in muscle fibres, which repair and grow stronger during recovery.

2. Benefits:

1. Increases lean muscle mass, boosting metabolic rate, and aiding weight management.
2. Strengthens bones and reduces the risk of osteoporosis.
3. Improves insulin sensitivity, reducing the risk of type 2 diabetes.

Flexibility and Balance: Preventing Injury and Enhancing Mobility

1. How It Works: Stretching and balance exercises improve joint range of motion, muscle elasticity, and proprioception.

2. Benefits:

1. Reduces muscle stiffness and soreness.
2. Prevents falls and injuries, particularly as you age.

Exercise and the Brain:

1. Regular physical activity increases the size of the hippocampus, the brain's centre for memory and learning.
2. Exercise reduces cortisol (the stress hormone) while increasing serotonin and dopamine, which regulate mood and motivation.

3. Sleep: The Body's Natural Reset Button

Sleep is essential for repairing the body, consolidating memories, and regulating emotions. Poor sleep disrupts physical, mental, and hormonal balance.

The Stages of Sleep:

1. Non-REM Sleep:

1. Stage 1: Light sleep, where the body begins to relax.
2. Stage 2: The heart rate slows, and brain activity decreases.
3. Stage 3: Deep sleep is crucial for physical recovery and immune system function.

2. REM Sleep:

1. The brain becomes highly active, dreaming occurs, and memories are consolidated.

The Sleep-Hormone Connection:

1. **Melatonin:** Released by the pineal gland, melatonin signals your body to prepare for sleep. It is influenced by light exposure, which is why limiting screens before bed is important.

2. **Cortisol:** High cortisol levels, often caused by stress, can interfere with falling and staying asleep.
3. **Growth Hormone:** Released during deep sleep, it aids in tissue repair, muscle growth, and immune health.

Sleep and Brain Health:

1. Sleep clears metabolic waste from the brain, reducing the risk of neurodegenerative diseases like Alzheimer's.
2. Sleep deprivation impairs the prefrontal cortex, which governs decision-making, focus, and emotional regulation.

Interconnectedness of Nutrition, Exercise, and Sleep

These three pillars don't operate in isolation; they amplify each other's benefits:

- **Exercise Improves Sleep:** Physical activity promotes deeper, more restorative sleep.
- **Sleep Enhances Exercise Recovery:** Quality sleep repairs muscles and replenishes energy, making workouts more effective.
- **Nutrition Fuels Both:** A balanced diet provides the energy needed for exercise and the nutrients required for recovery and brain health.

Example: A well-fed, well-rested body can handle the stress of a high-intensity workout better and recover faster.

The Science of Balance

Achieving balance means understanding your body's unique needs and creating a lifestyle that aligns with them. Here's how balance plays out:

Hormonal Harmony:

1. Nutrition, exercise, and sleep regulate hormones like insulin, cortisol, and serotonin, ensuring your body functions optimally.
2. Imbalance (e.g., lack of sleep or overtraining) disrupts this harmony, leading to fatigue, cravings, and stress.

Energy Allocation:

1. A balanced approach prevents burnout. For example, pairing moderate exercise with sufficient rest and proper nutrition ensures long-term sustainability.

Practical Applications of the Science

1. Nutrition:

1. Eat a high-protein meal after strength training to repair and build muscles.
2. Include magnesium-rich foods (like spinach or almonds) in your diet to support sleep.

2. Exercise:

1. Combine strength training with aerobic activities for holistic health.
2. Schedule workouts earlier in the day to avoid disrupting your sleep cycle.

3. Sleep:

1. Stick to a bedtime routine to regulate your circadian rhythm.
2. Use exercise as a natural way to reduce anxiety and prepare your body for restful sleep.

By understanding these scientific principles, you can create a personalised health and fitness plan that maximises your energy, focus, and resilience.

Strategies for Health and Fitness

Achieving optimal health and fitness requires a balanced approach that integrates nutrition, exercise, and sleep into your daily life. These strategies are designed to be practical, sustainable, and effective, ensuring that you can maintain your physical and mental well-being while pursuing your goals.

1. Nutrition Strategies: Fuelling Your Body and Mind

Proper nutrition is the cornerstone of good health. It provides the energy and nutrients needed for your body and brain to function efficiently.

a. Plan Your Meals for Balance

1. How It Helps: Ensures your diet includes essential macronutrients and micronutrients.

2. Action Steps:

1. Follow the "plate method": Fill half your plate with vegetables, a quarter with lean protein, and a quarter with whole grains.

2.   Prepare meals in advance to avoid unhealthy last-minute choices.

b. Control Portions Without Deprivation

1. How It Helps: Prevents overeating while allowing you to enjoy a variety of foods.

2. Action Steps:

1.   Use smaller plates and bowls to control portions.
2.   Practice mindful eating: Chew slowly, savour flavours, and stop when you feel satisfied.

C. Focus on Nutrient-Dense Foods

1. **How It Helps:** Provides more vitamins, minerals, and fibre while minimising empty calories.

2. **Action Steps:**

1.   Replace processed snacks with whole foods like fruits, nuts, or yogurt.
2.   Choose complex carbs (e.g., quinoa, sweet potatoes) over refined ones (e.g., white bread).

d. Stay Hydrated

1. How It Helps: Improves metabolism, brain function, and energy levels.

2. Action Steps:

1.   Carry a reusable water bottle and set reminders to drink water throughout the day.
2.   Infuse water with lemon or cucumber for added flavour.

Example: A busy professional preps weekly meals with grilled chicken, roasted vegetables, and brown rice, ensuring balanced nutrition without extra effort.

2. Exercise Strategies: Building Strength and Stamina

Regular physical activity is crucial for maintaining a healthy weight, reducing stress, and improving overall fitness.

a. Find an Exercise Routine You Enjoy

1. How It Helps: Increases consistency by making workouts fun and engaging.

2. Action Steps:

1. Try various activities (e.g. swimming, dancing, hiking) to find what you love.
2. Join group classes or sports teams to make exercise social and enjoyable.

B. Start Small and Build Gradually

1. How It Helps: Prevents burnout and reduces the risk of injury.

2. Action Steps:

1. Begin with 10–15 minutes of activity and increase duration and intensity over time.
2. Use beginner-friendly workout apps or follow online videos for guidance.

C. Incorporate Strength and Flexibility Training

- **How It Helps:** Supports muscle development, joint health, and mobility.

- **Action Steps:**

    o Include two strength-training sessions per week (e.g., lifting weights or bodyweight exercises).
    o Add yoga or stretching routines to improve flexibility and reduce stiffness.

D. Use Technology to Stay Motivated

1. How It Helps: Tracks progress and keeps you accountable.

2. Action Steps:

1. Use fitness apps like Strava or Fitbit to monitor activity levels.
2. Set daily step goals and celebrate milestones.

Example: A college student sets a goal of walking 10,000 steps daily and uses a pedometer app to track progress, gradually incorporating strength exercises twice a week.

3. Sleep Strategies: The Foundation of Recovery

Quality sleep is essential for muscle recovery, cognitive function, and emotional well-being. Prioritising rest helps you perform better in all areas of life.

a. Create a Consistent Sleep Schedule

1. How It Helps: Regulates your circadian rhythm, making it easier to fall and stay asleep.

2. Action Steps:

1. Go to bed and wake up at the same time every day, even on weekends.

2. Use an alarm not just for waking up but also for starting your bedtime routine.

b. Optimise Your Sleep Environment

1. How It Helps: Promotes relaxation and minimises disturbances.

2. Action Steps:

1. Keep your bedroom cool, dark, and quiet.
2. Invest in comfortable bedding and blackout curtains.

C. Develop a Wind-Down Routine

1. How It Helps: Signals your brain that it's time to relax and prepare for sleep.

2. Action Steps:

1. Avoid screens 1–2 hours before bedtime to reduce blue light exposure.
2. Engage in calming activities like reading, journaling, or meditation.

D. Avoid Stimulants Before Bed

1. **How It Helps:** Prevents interference with your body's ability to wind down.

2. **Action Steps:**

1. Limit caffeine intake after 2 pm.
2. Avoid heavy meals or intense exercise close to bedtime.

Example: A student struggling with late-night insomnia establishes a wind-down routine that includes journaling and meditation, improving sleep quality and focus.

4. Balancing the Three Pillars of Health

Achieving health and fitness isn't about excelling in just one area—it's about maintaining a balance between nutrition, exercise, and sleep.

a. Listen to Your Body

1. How It Helps: Helps you recognise when you need rest, recovery, or adjustments in your routine.

2. Action Steps:

1. Pay attention to hunger, fatigue, or soreness as cues to adjust your habits.
2. Take rest days when needed to avoid overtraining.

B. Use the 80/20 Rule

1. How It Helps: Ensures consistency without the pressure of perfection.

2. Action Steps:

1. Follow healthy habits 80% of the time while allowing flexibility for treats and relaxation.
2. Example: Enjoy a slice of cake at a celebration but maintain healthy meals the rest of the day.

c. Incorporate Active Recovery

1. How It Helps: Promotes recovery while keeping you active.

2. Action Steps:

1. Do light activities like walking or yoga on rest days to keep your body moving.

D. Plan Your Day Around Your Energy Levels

1. How It Helps: Matches tasks to your natural energy peaks for better productivity.

2. Action Steps:

1. Schedule workouts during times when you feel most energetic.
2. Eat lighter meals when you're less active and more substantial ones before or after workouts.

Example: A busy professional balances their routine by prioritising sleep, scheduling morning workouts, and meal prepping healthy lunches.

- Your body needs exercise to support recovery.
- Exercise enhances sleep quality and maintains physical strength.
- Sleep enables recovery, focus, and energy for daily activities.

By combining these strategies, you create a sustainable lifestyle that supports your long-term health, productivity, and happiness.

Case Studies: Real-Life Examples of Balanced Health

Case Study 1: James's Transformation Through Small Changes

James, a software developer, struggled with low energy due to a poor diet and lack of exercise. He started making small adjustments: swapping fast food for home-cooked meals, walking 10 minutes after lunch, and cutting screen time before bed. Over six months, James lost 20 pounds, felt more energetic, and became more productive at work.

Case Study 2: Maria's Busy-Professional Wellness Plan

Maria, a lawyer with long work hours, used time-blocking to incorporate fitness and meal prep into her schedule. She started waking up 30 minutes earlier to exercise and prepping healthy meals on Sundays. Her consistency improved her focus and reduced her stress levels.

Case Study 3: Anika's Journey to Better Sleep

Anika, a college student, was experiencing brain fog and irritability. By committing to a wind-down routine and limiting late-night social media use, she improved her sleep quality. Her academic performance and mood significantly improved within weeks.

Fun Activity: Design Your Fitness Circle

Draw a circle and divide it into three sections labelled nutrition, exercise, and sleep. Rate your current habits in each area on a scale of 1–10. Identify one action to improve each section and commit to it for the next week.

Exercises After Chapter 14

Exercise 1: Create a Weekly Health Plan

1. Plan your meals for the week, ensuring balance and variety.
2. Schedule three workout sessions, even if they're only 15 minutes long.
3. Set a consistent bedtime and track your sleep quality.

Exercise 2: The Hydration Challenge

Track your water intake daily for a week, aiming for at least eight glasses. Reflect on how staying hydrated affects your energy and focus.

Conclusion: Invest in Your Health

Your body is your greatest asset, and maintaining its well-being is essential for achieving your goals and enjoying life's journey. By focusing on balanced nutrition, regular exercise, and quality sleep, you can build the energy and resilience needed to become your best self.

Quote: "Health is not valued until sickness comes." – Thomas Fuller

CHAPTER 15

Giving Back

Creating Impact Through Community Service and Philanthropy

Why This Chapter Matters

Giving back isn't just about helping others—it's a transformative act that benefits the giver as much as the recipient. Contributing your time, skills, or resources to your community fosters personal growth, strengthens social bonds, and creates a ripple effect of positivity. In this chapter, we'll explore the profound value of community service and philanthropy, share inspiring stories of young philanthropists, and provide actionable steps to integrate giving back into your life.

Quote: "We make a living by what we get. We make a life by what we give." – Winston Churchill

The Science of Giving Back

The act of giving back, whether through community service, donations, or advocacy, has profound psychological, emotional, and even physiological benefits. Scientific research shows that altruistic behaviour is deeply embedded in human nature and contributes significantly to personal well-being and societal cohesion.

1. The Psychology of Altruism

Altruism, or the selfless concern for the well-being of others, is a fundamental aspect of human behaviour. It is hardwired into our brains, influencing how we interact with others and how we derive meaning from life.

How Altruism Benefits You:

1. Helper's High: When you engage in acts of kindness, your brain releases dopamine and endorphins, creating feelings of happiness and euphoria.
2. Oxytocin Boost: Altruism increases levels of oxytocin, the "love hormone," which fosters trust, empathy, and social bonding.
3. Reduced Stress: Helping others lowers cortisol levels, reducing stress and promoting emotional resilience.

Practical Example:

A study published in *Social Psychological and Personality Science* found that people who performed daily acts of kindness reported higher levels of happiness and lower levels of stress after just 10 days.

2. Neurobiology of Giving

Giving triggers activation in the brain's mesolimbic reward system, the same pathway that responds to pleasurable activities like eating or exercising. Key areas of the brain involved include:

1. Ventral Striatum: Linked to reward and motivation, this region lights up when you give or volunteer.
2. Prefrontal Cortex: Associated with decision-making, it reinforces the idea that altruistic actions are meaningful and valuable.

How This Shapes Behaviour:

The reward system encourages repeated acts of generosity by associating them with positive emotions. This explains why people who regularly give back often report feeling more fulfilled.

Practical Tip:

Make giving a habit—volunteer weekly or set up recurring donations—to continually activate this reward system and reinforce altruistic behaviour.

3. The Ripple Effect of Giving

Acts of kindness don't just benefit the giver and recipient, they create a ripple effect that influences entire communities. This phenomenon, known as prosocial contagion, explains how generosity spreads from person to person.

Scientific Insight:

Research published in *Proceedings of the National Academy of Sciences* demonstrated that witnessing or experiencing an act of kindness makes individuals more likely to "pay it forward" by helping someone else.

Example:

If you donate to a friend's charity fundraiser, that friend may feel inspired to contribute more time or resources to the cause, creating a chain of generosity.

4. Giving and Emotional Health

Helping others has a significant impact on emotional well-being. It can combat feelings of loneliness, anxiety, and depression by fostering a sense of connection and purpose.

Key Emotional Benefits of Giving:

1. Improved Mood: Acts of kindness elevate levels of serotonin, a neurotransmitter that regulates mood and feelings of contentment.
2. Sense of Purpose: Volunteering or contributing to a cause provides a sense of direction and fulfilment.
3. Reduced Isolation: Giving back connects you to others, fostering a sense of belonging and community.

Practical Example:

A study in *The Journal of Social Psychology* found that participants who performed five acts of kindness a week experienced a significant increase in overall happiness.

5. Physical Health Benefits

Engaging in acts of giving not only improves mental health but also has tangible physical benefits.

How Giving Impacts Physical Health:

1. Reduced Blood Pressure: Altruistic behaviour has been linked to lower blood pressure, reducing the risk of cardiovascular diseases.
2. Strengthened Immune System: Acts of kindness and social connection promote immune system function, making you less susceptible to illness.

3. Increased Longevity: A study in *Health Psychology* found that individuals who regularly volunteered had a 44% lower mortality rate compared to those who didn't.

Practical Tip:

Combine physical activity with giving back, such as participating in charity runs or community clean-ups, to amplify these health benefits.

6. Evolutionary Perspective on Altruism

From an evolutionary standpoint, altruism played a crucial role in the survival of early human societies.

Why Altruism Evolved:

1. Strength in Numbers: Helping others ensured stronger group cohesion, which increased the chances of survival for the entire community.
2. Reciprocity: Generosity often leads to reciprocal acts, creating mutual support networks.

Modern Implications:

While the survival pressures of ancient times have lessened, the ingrained tendency to help others remains, shaping human behaviour and societal structures.

7. The Long-Term Impact of Giving

Beyond the immediate emotional and physical benefits, giving back creates long-lasting positive effects.

Building Resilience:

Acts of kindness improve emotional resilience, helping you cope better with stress and adversity.

Enhancing Relationships:

Generosity strengthens social bonds, making personal and professional relationships more meaningful and rewarding.

Creating a Legacy:

Philanthropy and community service allow you to leave a lasting positive impact on the world.

Scientific Summary: Why Giving Back Matters

Benefit	Scientific Basis	Example of Insight
Increased Happiness	Dopamine and oxytocin are released during acts of kindness.	Helper's high from volunteering at a shelter.
Reduced Stress	Cortisol reduction linked to altruistic behaviour.	Stress relief after organising a charity event.
Stronger Community	The ripple effect and prosocial contagion.	Paying it forward inspires others to do the same.
Better Health	Lower blood pressure and improved immune function.	Volunteering reduces heart disease risk.
Sense of Purpose	Activation of the prefrontal cortex.	Feeling fulfilled after mentoring a student.

How to Leverage the Science of Giving Back

1. Start Small: Simple acts like smiling at someone or holding the door open can trigger positive emotions and encourage prosocial behaviour.
2. Be Consistent: Regularly engaging in giving activities creates habits that reinforce happiness and fulfilment.
3. Track Your Impact: Reflect on the outcomes of your efforts—whether it's seeing a clean park after a community clean-up or knowing your donation funded a specific project.

By understanding the scientific principles behind giving back, you can harness its benefits to enhance your well-being and contribute meaningfully to the world.

Ways to Give Back

1. Volunteer Your Time.

Time is one of the most valuable resources you can give. Volunteering not only supports a cause but also helps you develop new skills and meet like-minded people.

How to Start:

1. Identify causes you're passionate about (e.g., education, environmental conservation).
2. Research local organisations or online platforms like Volunteer Match.
3. Commit to a regular schedule or participate in one-time events.

Example: A student volunteers at a community tutoring programme, helping younger students succeed while building leadership skills.

2. Donate Skills or Expertise

If you have a specialised skill or talent, consider using it to support a cause.

How to Start:

1. Offer pro bono services to non-profits or community groups.
2. Teach a workshop or mentor someone in need.
3. Use creative skills to raise awareness, such as designing posters or creating social media campaigns.

Example: A graphic designer creates promotional materials for a local animal shelter, increasing adoption rates.

3. Financial Philanthropy

Monetary donations, no matter the amount, can make a significant impact when directed towards meaningful causes.

How to Start:

- Research organisations with transparent practices and proven impact (e.g., Charity Navigator).
- Set aside a portion of your income for charitable giving.
- Consider crowdfunding platforms like GoFundMe to support individuals or grassroots initiatives.

Example: A young professional donates a percentage of their monthly salary to a scholarship fund for underprivileged students.

4. Organise Community Events

Take the initiative to bring people together for a common cause.

How to Start:

1. Plan a local clean-up, book drive, or charity run.
2. Partner with community organisations or businesses to amplify the event's reach.
3. Encourage friends and family to participate, fostering a sense of community.

Example: A group of college students organises a clothing drive, collecting and distributing winter coats to homeless shelters.

5. Advocate for Causes You Believe In.

Raising awareness about issues you care about can inspire others to take action.

How to Start:

1. Use social media to share information and resources.
2. Write to local representatives or join advocacy groups.
3. Attend protests, rallies, or community meetings.

Example: An environmentalist shares tips for reducing plastic waste on Instagram, encouraging followers to adopt eco-friendly habits.

Case Studies: Inspiring Young Philanthropists

Case Study 1: Malala Yousafzai's Fight for Education

Malala Yousafzai, the youngest Nobel Peace Prize laureate, advocates for girls' education worldwide. Despite facing violence and adversity, she founded the Malala Fund to provide education for millions of girls in underserved regions.

Key Takeaway: Passion and resilience can turn personal challenges into a global impact.

Case Study 2: Ryan's Well Foundation

At the age of six, Ryan Hreljac learned about the lack of clean water in developing countries. Determined to make a difference, he started fundraising to build a well in Uganda. This small act grew into the Ryan's Well Foundation, which has since funded over 1,600 water projects worldwide.

Key Takeaway: Age is no barrier to making a significant difference; start small and dream big.

Case Study 3: Greta Thunberg's Climate Activism

Greta Thunberg, a teenager from Sweden, began a school strike for climate action, which evolved into a global movement. Her advocacy has inspired millions to join protests, demand policy changes, and adopt sustainable practices.

Key Takeaway: Advocacy and awareness can ignite global change when rooted in passion and commitment.

Fun Activity: Your Giving Back Blueprint

1. Objective: Create a personalised plan for giving back based on your strengths, interests, and resources.

2. Steps:

   1. List three causes you care about (e.g. animal welfare, education, mental health).
   2. Identify one way you can contribute to each cause (e.g. volunteering, donating, organising events).

3. Commit to taking action on one cause this month.

Exercises After Chapter 15

Exercise 1: Random Acts of Kindness Challenge

1. Perform one random act of kindness each day for a week (e.g., buying coffee for a stranger or complimenting a coworker).
2. Reflect on how these acts made you and others feel.

Exercise 2: Volunteer Planning Worksheet

1. Research local volunteering opportunities.
2. Write down one opportunity that aligns with your skills and interests.
3. Schedule a time to participate and commit to following through.

Exercise 3: Philanthropy Journal

1. Choose a charity or cause to support financially.
2. Write down why this cause matters to you and track your donations over time.
3. Reflect on the impact your contributions have made.

Conclusion: The Power of Contribution

Giving back is not just an act of generosity—it's a way to connect with others, foster personal growth, and create lasting change. By contributing your time, skills, or resources, you can inspire others and leave a positive mark on the world.

Quote: "No one has ever become poor by giving." – Anne Frank

Part V

The Big Picture

CHAPTER 16

Balancing Ambition and Patience

How to Aim High While Remaining Grounded

Why This Chapter Matters

Ambition fuels your drive to achieve goals, while patience ensures you navigate the journey with resilience and clarity. Striking the right balance between these two forces is critical for sustainable success. Without ambition, you risk stagnation. Without patience, you risk burnout. This chapter explores how to set high aspirations while staying grounded, avoiding the common traps of impatience, frustration, and overexertion.

Quote: "Patience is not the ability to wait, but the ability to keep a good attitude while waiting." – Joyce Meyer

The Science of Balancing Ambition and Patience

1. The Role of Dopamine in Motivation and Ambition

Dopamine, often referred to as the "motivation molecule," drives goal-directed behaviour. Every time you achieve a small milestone, your brain releases dopamine, reinforcing the effort and encouraging you to strive for more.

The Challenge:

Dopamine can create a cycle of constant craving for success, leading to impatience and dissatisfaction if goals aren't achieved quickly.

How to Balance:

1. Break larger goals into smaller milestones to maintain a steady dopamine reward.
2. Celebrate progress, no matter how small, to stay motivated without becoming impatient.

2. Patience and the Prefrontal Cortex

The prefrontal cortex, responsible for decision-making and emotional regulation, helps you manage the tension between ambition and patience. Developing patience strengthens this part of the brain, enhancing your ability to delay gratification and persevere through challenges.

Practical Application:

Engage in activities like mindfulness meditation to train your prefrontal cortex and improve emotional control.

3. The Growth Mindset Connection

Ambition aligns closely with a growth mindset—the belief that abilities can be developed through effort. Patience complements this by fostering resilience when progress feels slow.

How to Balance:

1. Embrace setbacks as learning opportunities rather than signs of failure.
2. Focus on the process rather than obsessing over immediate results.

Strategies for Balancing Ambition and Patience

1. Set SMART Goals (Specific, Measurable, Achievable, Relevant, Time-Bound).

Ambition without clarity leads to frustration. SMART goals break down your aspirations into actionable steps.

How to Use SMART Goals:

1. Specific: Clearly define what you want to achieve.

   Example: "Increase my monthly savings by 20% in six months."

2. Measurable: Track progress to stay motivated.
3. Achievable: Ensure the goal is realistic based on your current resources and abilities.
4. Relevant: Align the goal with your long-term vision.
5. Time-Bound: Set a deadline to create urgency without pressure.

Example: A college student aiming for a top-tier internship creates a SMART goal: "Apply to five internships in my field within the next two months."

2. Embrace the Power of Incremental Progress.

Ambition often focuses on big leaps, but meaningful growth happens through consistent small steps.

How to Focus on Progress:

- Track daily or weekly achievements to reinforce a sense of accomplishment.
- Reflect on how far you've come instead of fixating on how far you have to go.

Example: A writer aspiring to complete a novel commits to writing 500 words daily. By the end of the year, they will have a full manuscript.

3. Develop Emotional Resilience

Ambition can lead to frustration when obstacles arise, but resilience helps you remain patient and adapt to challenges.

Ways to Build Resilience:

1. Practice Gratitude: Shift focus from what you lack to what you've achieved.
2. Reframe Failure: View setbacks as part of the learning process.
3. Maintain Perspective: Remember that long-term success often requires temporary sacrifices.

Example: An entrepreneur faces rejection from investors but uses the feedback to refine their pitch and ultimately secures funding.

4. Practice Mindfulness and Stress Management.

Patience is tested when stress levels are high. Mindfulness can help you stay present and avoid being overwhelmed by future-focused ambitions.

Mindfulness Techniques:

1. Deep Breathing: Take slow, deep breaths to calm your nervous system.
2. Meditation: Spend 5–10 minutes daily focusing on your breath or a calming visualisation.
3. Journaling: Reflect on your thoughts and feelings to gain clarity.

Example: A student preparing for exams uses mindfulness to stay calm and focused, reducing anxiety about their future performance.

5. Balance Ambition with Self-Compassion.

Being ambitious often comes with high expectations, which can lead to self-criticism. Self-compassion helps you maintain patience by treating yourself kindly during setbacks.

How to Practice Self-Compassion:

1. Acknowledge Struggles: Recognise that challenges are a natural part of growth.
2. Speak Kindly to Yourself: Replace self-critical thoughts with encouraging ones.
3. Take Breaks: Rest isn't laziness—it's essential for long-term productivity.

Example: A programmer struggling to debug their code steps away for a walk, returns with a clear mind, and solves the problem more efficiently.

Case Studies: Balancing Ambition and Patience

Case Study 1: Elon Musk's Long-Term Vision

Background:

Elon Musk, a visionary entrepreneur, is known for his ambitious goals, such as colonising Mars with SpaceX and transitioning the world to sustainable energy with Tesla. These aspirations require groundbreaking innovation, immense resources, and years of perseverance.

Challenges:

1. SpaceX faced multiple failed rocket launches in its early years, leading to financial strain and scepticism from investors.
2. Tesla struggled with production delays, technical challenges, and intense public scrutiny during the rollout of the Model 3.

Balancing Ambition and Patience:

1. Ambition: Musk's ultimate goal is to make life multi-planetary, a vision that goes beyond immediate rewards.
2. Patience: Despite setbacks, Musk focuses on incremental progress. Each failed rocket launch was analysed meticulously, leading to improvements in design and technology. Similarly, Tesla's production "hell" taught valuable lessons about scaling manufacturing.

Outcome:

1. SpaceX achieved historic milestones, such as successfully landing reusable rockets and launching the first private crewed mission to the International Space Station.
2. Tesla became a global leader in electric vehicles, with record-breaking sales and market value.

Key Takeaway:

Ambition requires a willingness to tackle audacious goals, but patience ensures resilience in the face of inevitable setbacks. Musk's ability to focus on long-term success while learning from short-term failures demonstrates the power of balancing these forces.

Case Study 2: J.K. Rowling's Journey to Publishing

Background:

J.K. Rowling, the author of the *Harry Potter* series, began writing the story during a challenging period in her life. As a single mother living on government assistance, she faced financial hardship and uncertainty about her future.

Challenges:

1. Rowling's manuscript for *Harry Potter and the Philosopher's Stone* was rejected by 12 publishers before being accepted by Bloomsbury.
2. She experienced self-doubt and feared her story might never reach readers.

Balancing Ambition and Patience:

1. Ambition: Rowling believed in her story's potential and maintained her determination to see it published, despite numerous rejections.
2. Patience: She persevered through the rejection process, revising her manuscript and continuing to query publishers. She also remained focused on her craft, working on subsequent books in the series.

Outcome:

1. Once published, *Harry Potter* became a global phenomenon, selling over 500 million copies and inspiring movies, merchandise, and theme parks.
2. Rowling transitioned from financial instability to becoming one of the wealthiest and most influential authors in history.

Key Takeaway:

Success often requires navigating rejection and failure. Rowling's story highlights how patience and unwavering ambition can turn obstacles into stepping stones for extraordinary achievements.

Case Study 3: Maria's Academic Growth

Background:

Maria, a high school student from a low-income family, dreamed of attending a prestigious university to pursue a career in medicine. However, her grades were average, and she struggled with subjects like math and chemistry.

Challenges:

1. Maria faced self-doubt, feeling she might not be capable of achieving her academic goals.
2. Limited resources for tutoring and extracurricular opportunities made her journey even more challenging.

Balancing Ambition and Patience:

1. Ambition: Maria set a long-term goal to improve her grades, excel in standardised tests, and secure scholarships.
2. Patience: Instead of expecting immediate results, she focused on incremental improvements.
   1. She created a study schedule, dedicating time to her weakest subjects.
   2. She sought mentorship from a teacher who guided her through difficult concepts.
   3. She practised mindfulness techniques to manage stress and maintain focus.

Outcome:

1. Over two years, Maria's grades steadily improved, and she scored in the top percentile on her SATs.
2. She earned a full scholarship to her dream university and became the first in her family to attend college.

Key Takeaway:

Ambition provides the vision for where you want to go, but patience ensures that you take consistent, deliberate steps to get there. Maria's story shows that success is built on perseverance and incremental progress.

Case Study 4: A Start-Up's Path to Success

Background:

Alex and Priya, two entrepreneurs, co-founded a start-up to develop an app that simplifies personal budgeting. They were passionate about financial literacy and envisioned their app helping millions of people manage their money.

Challenges:

1. Early versions of the app were plagued with bugs and received poor user reviews.
2. They struggled to secure funding, as investors were sceptical about the app's potential in a crowded market.

Balancing Ambition and Patience:

1. Ambition: Alex and Priya believed in their mission and set a high goal: reaching 1 million active users within three years.
2. Patience: They used negative feedback to refine the app, releasing updates that addressed user concerns. They also continued pitching to investors, learning from rejections, and improving their presentation.

Outcome:

1. Within three years, the app gained traction and achieved 1.5 million active users, becoming a top-rated financial app.
2. They secured a round of funding that allowed them to expand their team and introduce new features.

Key Takeaway:

Ambitious goals require the patience to iterate, learn, and grow. Alex and Priya's ability to stay grounded while pursuing their vision enabled their start-up to thrive.

Case Study 5: Simone Biles' Journey to Olympic Gold

Background:

Simone Biles, widely regarded as one of the greatest gymnasts of all time, set her sights on becoming an Olympic champion from a young age. Her journey required immense dedication, rigorous training, and mental resilience.

Challenges:

- Early in her career, Biles struggled with consistency and faced intense competition on the global stage.
- She also dealt with the physical and mental toll of training, including injuries and burnout.

Balancing Ambition and Patience:

1. Ambition: Biles maintained a high standard for herself, continually pushing the boundaries of what was possible in gymnastics.
2. Patience: She understood the importance of recovery, both physically and mentally. She worked closely with her coaches to refine her routines and waited for the right opportunities to debut new, groundbreaking skills.

Outcome:

1. Biles became a four-time Olympic gold medallist and 19-time World Champion, redefining the sport with her innovative moves.
2. Her story of balancing ambition with self-care inspired millions, particularly when she prioritised her mental health during the Tokyo Olympics.

Key Takeaway:

Balancing ambition with patience allows you to pursue excellence without compromising well-being. Simone Biles exemplifies the power of persistence and self-awareness in achieving greatness.

Lessons from the Case Studies.

1. Ambition Requires a Long-Term Vision:

1. Success stories like Elon Musk's and Simone Biles' highlight the importance of thinking beyond immediate results.

2. Patience Cultivates Resilience:

1. From Maria's academic growth to J.K. Rowling's publishing journey, patience enables individuals to overcome challenges and stay focused on their goals.

3. Iteration and Adaptation Are Key:

1. Alex and Priya's start-up journey underscores the value of learning from mistakes and refining your approach.

4. Success Is a Marathon, Not a Sprint:

1.   Each of these stories demonstrates that the path to success is rarely linear and requires both ambition and patience to navigate.

Fun Activity: Ambition-Patience Scale

1. Objective: Assess your current balance between ambition and patience.

2. Instructions:

1.   Draw a balance scale with "Ambition" on one side and "Patience" on the other.
2.   Write actions or behaviours you associate with each side.
3.   Reflect on whether the scale is tilted too far in one direction and identify one change you can make to achieve balance.

Exercises After Chapter 16

Exercise 1: Define Your Ambitions

1.   Write down three big goals you want to achieve.
2.   Break each goal into smaller, actionable steps.
3.   Set a realistic timeline for each step.

Exercise 2: Build a Patience Practice

1.   Identify situations where you feel impatient.
2.   Practice deep breathing or mindfulness in those moments.
3.   Write about how patience influenced the outcome.

Exercise 3: Celebrate Incremental Wins

1. List three recent small accomplishments related to your goals.
2. Reflect on how each step contributes to your larger vision.

Conclusion: The Art of Balanced Growth

Balancing ambition and patience is a lifelong skill. By aiming high while remaining grounded, you can achieve your goals without sacrificing your well-being or losing sight of the bigger picture. Success is not just about reaching the summit—it's about appreciating the journey and growing along the way.

Quote: "Ambition is the path to success. Persistence is the vehicle you arrive in." – Bill Bradley.

CHAPTER 17

Leaving a Legacy

Thinking Long-Term: What Will You Be Remembered For?

Why This Chapter Matters

Leaving a legacy isn't about fame or fortune; it's about the impact you make on others and the world. Your actions, values, and contributions create ripples that can influence generations. By thinking long-term and aligning your life with a meaningful purpose, you can ensure that your legacy reflects the best version of yourself.

This chapter delves into the concept of legacy, explores the importance of intentional living, and shares inspiring examples of individuals who have left indelible marks on history.

Quote: "The great use of life is to spend it for something that will outlast it." – William James.

The Science of Legacy

1. The Psychology of Legacy

The desire to leave a legacy is a fundamental aspect of human nature, often tied to the need for meaning and purpose. This drive is rooted in generativity, a concept introduced by psychologist Erik Erikson. Generativity is the act of contributing to the well-being of future generations, often through mentorship, creativity, or community service.

How Legacy Impacts Mental Health:

1. Sense of Purpose: Knowing your actions contribute to something greater enhances emotional well-being.
2. Reduced Regret: A legacy-focused mindset encourages intentional choices, minimising end-of-life regrets.
3. Enhanced Resilience: Striving for a long-term impact fosters perseverance during challenges.

Practical Tip: Reflect on what you want your life to stand for. This clarity can guide your decisions and priorities.

2. The Ripple Effect of Legacy

Legacy often extends beyond the individual. Your actions can inspire others to create a positive impact, resulting in a ripple effect.

Scientific Insight:

Studies in social psychology suggest that role models significantly influence others' behaviour, especially within families and communities.

Example: A teacher who mentors a struggling student not only changes that student's life but may also inspire them to help others in the future.

Strategies for Creating a Lasting Legacy

1. Define Your Core Values

Legacy begins with understanding what matters most to you. Your values act as the foundation for the actions and decisions that shape how you'll be remembered.

How to Define Core Values:

1. Reflect on moments when you felt proud or fulfilled.
2. Identify recurring themes in your passions, goals, and achievements.
3. Write a personal mission statement that aligns with these values.

Example: A business leader might prioritise integrity and sustainability, ensuring their company practices reflect these principles.

2. Contribute to Others' Lives

Helping others is one of the most impactful ways to leave a legacy. Whether through mentorship, charity, or sharing knowledge, acts of generosity create a ripple effect of positivity.

How to Start:

1. Volunteer in areas where you can make a meaningful difference.
2. Share your expertise with younger generations or peers.
3. Offer support to friends, family, and community members during times of need.

Example: Fred Rogers (*Mister Rogers' Neighbourhood*) left a legacy of kindness and empathy by dedicating his life to educating and comforting children.

3. Create Something That Outlasts You

Building or creating something tangible can ensure your legacy endures. This could be a work of art, a business, or even a tradition within your family.

Examples:

1. Writers and Artists: Books, music, and paintings that inspire future generations.
2. Entrepreneurs: Companies that continue to innovate and contribute to society.
3. Philanthropists: Foundations that address critical issues.

Example: Andrew Carnegie's legacy lives on through the libraries he funded, which continue to provide access to education.

4. Focus on Relationships

Your relationships often define how you'll be remembered. The love, support, and guidance you give to others leave an emotional legacy that far outweighs material achievements.

How to Strengthen Relationships:

1. Prioritise quality time with loved ones.
2. Be a role model for integrity, kindness, and humility.
3. Offer mentorship or guidance to younger generations.

Example: Family matriarchs and patriarchs often leave legacies of wisdom and resilience through their storytelling and leadership.

5. Think Long-Term in Your Decisions

Legacy-minded individuals often consider how their actions today will affect the future.

How to Practice Long-Term Thinking:

1. Set goals that align with your vision for the impact you want to make.
2. Consider the environmental, social, and ethical implications of your choices.
3. Invest in causes, businesses, or projects that align with your values.

Example: Greta Thunberg's activism is rooted in ensuring a sustainable planet for future generations.

Inspiring Historical Examples of Legacy

Case Study 1: Marie Curie – Legacy of Scientific Discovery

Background:

Marie Curie was a physicist and chemist who conducted pioneering research on radioactivity. Her discoveries of polonium and radium revolutionised science and medicine. Despite facing immense challenges, including limited opportunities for women in academia, Curie's work laid the foundation for advancements in cancer treatment and nuclear energy.

Challenges:

1. As a woman in late 19th and early 20th-century Europe, Curie faced discrimination and scepticism from male colleagues.
2. Financial constraints made it difficult for her to secure laboratory resources early in her career.
3. Prolonged exposure to radioactive materials caused health issues, yet she continued her research.

Legacy:

1. Curie was the first woman to win a Nobel Prize and remains the only person to win Nobel Prizes in two different scientific fields (Physics and Chemistry).
2. Her discoveries led to the development of X-ray machines and radiation therapy, saving countless lives.
3. The Marie Curie charity, established in her honour, continues to provide care and support for people living with terminal illnesses.

Key Takeaway: Passion and perseverance can create legacies that transform industries and improve humanity.

Case Study 2: Nelson Mandela – Legacy of Forgiveness and Reconciliation

Background:

Nelson Mandela, South Africa's first Black president, played a pivotal role in ending apartheid—a system of institutionalised racial segregation and discrimination. Mandela's leadership exemplified forgiveness, unity, and resilience.

Challenges:

1. Mandela spent 27 years in prison for his activism against apartheid.
2. Upon his release, he faced the monumental task of uniting a deeply divided nation.

Legacy:

1. Mandela led South Africa through a peaceful transition from apartheid to democracy.
2. His emphasis on reconciliation inspired the Truth and Reconciliation Commission, which allowed victims and perpetrators of apartheid-era crimes to share their stories.
3. Mandela became a global symbol of peace and justice, with initiatives like Mandela Day encouraging acts of kindness and community service worldwide.

Key Takeaway: A legacy of compassion and forgiveness can heal communities and inspire global respect.

Case Study 3: Jane Goodall – Legacy of Conservation

Background:

Jane Goodall is a renowned primatologist and anthropologist who revolutionised the study of animal behaviour. Her groundbreaking work with chimpanzees at Gombe Stream National Park in Tanzania challenged traditional beliefs about the relationship between humans and animals.

Challenges:

1. Goodall had no formal scientific training when she began her research.

2. Her findings, such as chimpanzees using tools, faced scepticism from the scientific community.

Legacy:

1. Goodall founded the Jane Goodall Institute, which promotes conservation and animal welfare worldwide.
2. She launched Roots & Shoots, a global youth programme that empowers young people to create sustainable change in their communities.
3. Her advocacy has inspired millions to protect wildlife and ecosystems.

Key Takeaway: A commitment to protecting the planet ensures a legacy that benefits future generations.

Case Study 4: Malala Yousafzai – Legacy of Education Advocacy

Background:

Malala Yousafzai, a Pakistani activist for girls' education, survived a Taliban assassination attempt at the age of 15. Her courage and determination have made her a global symbol of the fight for education rights.

Challenges:

1. Malala faced death threats from the Taliban for her outspoken advocacy.
2. After the attack, she endured a long recovery process while continuing her activism.

Legacy:

1. Malala became the youngest Nobel Peace Prize laureate at 17.

2. Through the Malala Fund, she has supported education initiatives in countries like Afghanistan, Nigeria, and Syria.
3. Her autobiography, *I Am Malala*, has inspired readers worldwide to stand up for their rights.

Key Takeaway: Even at a young age, focusing on a cause you're passionate about can create a far-reaching legacy.

Case Study 5: Andrew Carnegie – Legacy of Philanthropy

Background:

Andrew Carnegie, a Scottish-American industrialist, rose from poverty to become one of the wealthiest men in history. He believed in the principle of giving back and dedicated much of his fortune to philanthropy.

Challenges:

1. Carnegie faced criticism for the harsh working conditions in his steel factories during the early stages of his career.
2. Transitioning from a profit-driven businessman to a philanthropist required a shift in mindset and priorities.

Legacy:

- Carnegie donated over $350 million (equivalent to billions today) to causes such as education, science, and public libraries.
- His funding established over 2,500 libraries worldwide, giving countless individuals access to knowledge.

- Institutions like Carnegie Mellon University and the Carnegie Endowment for International Peace continue to advance education and global cooperation.

Key Takeaway: Wealth is most impactful when used to empower and uplift others.

Case Study 6: Fred Rogers – Legacy of Kindness and Empathy

Background:

Fred Rogers, the beloved host of *Mister Rogers' Neighbourhood*, dedicated his life to educating children about emotional intelligence, kindness, and acceptance. His calm demeanour and thoughtful lessons left an enduring mark on generations.

Challenges:

1. Rogers faced criticism for his unconventional approach to children's programming, which focused on gentle, slow-paced content.
2. He addressed difficult topics like divorce, racism, and grief at a time when such issues were rarely discussed with children.

Legacy:

1. *Mister Rogers' Neighbourhood* became one of the most iconic children's television shows, influencing millions of viewers.
2. His emphasis on kindness and understanding continues to resonate through initiatives like the Fred Rogers Centre.

Key Takeaway: Simple, consistent acts of kindness can create a legacy that touches countless lives.

Lessons from the Case Studies.

1. Diverse Paths, Common Purpose: Whether through science, activism, philanthropy, or kindness, these individuals created legacies by aligning their actions with their values.
2. Resilience in the Face of Adversity: Each case study demonstrates that perseverance and patience are essential for building a lasting legacy.
3. Ripple Effect of Impact: The influence of these legacies extends beyond the individual, inspiring others to contribute positively to society.

Fun Activity: Your Legacy Map

- Objective: Reflect on how you want to be remembered and create a plan to align your actions with your vision.
- Steps:

  o Divide a piece of paper into three sections: Personal Legacy, Professional Legacy, and Community Legacy.
  o Write down actions, values, or projects you want to be associated with in each category.
  o Choose one actionable step to work on this month to move closer to your legacy goals.

Exercises After Chapter 17

Exercise 1: Define Your Legacy Statement

1. Write a one-sentence statement summarising what you want to be remembered for.
2. Reflect on whether your current actions align with this vision.

Exercise 2: Identify Role Models

1. List three people whose legacies inspire you.
2. Note the qualities or actions that made their legacies impactful.
3. Think about how you can incorporate these qualities into your life.

Exercise 3: Start a Legacy Project

1. Choose a project aligned with your passions (e.g., starting a blog, planting a community garden, mentoring someone).
2. Set measurable goals to track progress and impact.

Conclusion: Living with Purpose

Leaving a legacy is about making choices today that reflect the person you want to be remembered as tomorrow. By focusing on your values, relationships, and contributions, you can create a meaningful impact that outlives you.

Quote: "Your legacy is every life you've touched." – Maya Angelou

CHAPTER 18

The Road Ahead

Reflecting on the Journey and What Comes After 25

Why This Chapter Matters

Turning 26 is not the end of the road; it's a new beginning. The lessons and experiences from the transformative years between 18 and 25 serve as a foundation for the rest of your life. This chapter invites you to reflect on your journey, assess your growth, and plan for what comes next. By setting intentional goals for the years ahead, you can continue to build a life that aligns with your values, passions, and aspirations.

Quote: "Life is a journey, not a destination. The road ahead is always more important than the road behind." – Ralph Waldo Emerson.

Reflecting on the Journey: Lessons from 18-25

1. Growth Through Challenges

The years between 18 and 25 are filled with challenges, from navigating independence to establishing your identity.

These experiences teach resilience, adaptability, and problem-solving.

Reflection Questions:

1. What were the biggest challenges you faced, and how did you overcome them?
2. What did these challenges teach you about yourself and your strengths?

Example: A graduate struggling to find a job during economic uncertainty learns to pivot and upskill, discovering a passion for a new field.

2. Milestones and Achievements

This period is often marked by significant milestones, such as completing education, starting a career, or forming meaningful relationships. Recognising and celebrating these achievements fosters gratitude and motivation.

Reflection Questions:

1. What milestones are you most proud of?
2. How have these achievements shaped your goals and values?

Example: A young entrepreneur reflects on launching their first business, acknowledging the hard work and creativity it took to succeed.

3. Lessons from Failures

Failure is an inevitable part of growth. The key is to view failures as opportunities for learning and improvement rather than as setbacks.

Reflection Questions:

1. What failures taught you the most valuable lessons?
2. How did these experiences influence your approach to challenges and goals?

Example: A student who initially struggles with time management learns to create effective schedules and routines, boosting productivity and confidence.

The Road Ahead: Planning for Life After 25

1. Embrace Lifelong Learning.

The journey of growth doesn't stop at 25. Cultivating a mindset of continuous learning ensures that you remain adaptable and open to new opportunities.

Action Steps:

- Explore online courses or certifications to expand your skills.
- Read books and engage with content that challenges your perspective.
- Stay curious and seek out new experiences.

Example: A professional enrols in leadership courses to prepare for a management role, fostering both personal and career development.

2. Set Long-Term Goals

While the 18–25 period often focuses on short-term milestones, your late twenties and beyond allow for a broader vision.

How to Set Long-Term Goals:

1. Envision Your Future: Where do you see yourself in 5, 10, or 20 years?
2. Break It Down: Divide larger goals into actionable steps with timelines.
3. Stay Flexible: Reassess and adjust goals as your circumstances and priorities evolve.

Example: An aspiring writer sets a goal to publish a novel within the next five years, dedicating time weekly to writing and research.

3. Build Financial Independence

The years after 25 are an excellent time to focus on financial stability, which provides freedom and security.

Steps to Build Financial Independence:

1. Create a budget that prioritises savings and investments.
2. Pay down debt strategically, starting with high-interest loans.
3. Explore additional income streams, such as freelancing or investing.

Example: A professional commits to saving 20% of their income, investing in index funds, and building an emergency fund.

4. Strengthen Relationships

The relationships you nurture after 25 will play a significant role in your happiness and success.

How to Build Meaningful Relationships:

1. Invest time in friendships and family bonds.
2. Seek out mentors and like-minded peers.
3. Communicate openly and authentically.

Example: A young professional joins a networking group to connect with others in their industry, gaining both friendships and career opportunities.

5. Leave Room for the Unexpected

Life rarely goes exactly as planned. Embracing uncertainty and being open to change can lead to unexpected growth and opportunities.

Practical Tips:

1. Adopt a flexible mindset: View change as a chance to grow.
2. Cultivate resilience: Learn to adapt to setbacks and find solutions.
3. Take calculated risks: Step out of your comfort zone to discover new passions and paths.

Example: A designer who loses a job during an industry downturn starts freelancing, eventually discovering a passion for working with startups.

Exercises After Chapter 18

Exercise 1: Reflect on Your Journey

1. Write a letter to your 18-year-old self, reflecting on the lessons you've learned and the growth you've experienced.

2. Identify three key moments that defined your 18–25 journey and explain why they were significant.

Exercise 2: Create a Vision Board for Life After 25

1. Gather images, quotes, and symbols that represent your goals and dreams.
2. Arrange them on a board or digital platform as a visual reminder of your aspirations.
3. Review your vision board regularly to stay inspired.

Exercise 3: Set Goals for 26+

1. Choose one area of focus: career, health, relationships, or personal growth.
2. Write down one short-term goal (6 months), one medium-term goal (5 years), and one long-term goal (10 years).
3. Outline the steps you'll take to achieve each goal.

Conclusion: Embracing the Next Chapter

The journey beyond 25 is an opportunity to build on the foundation you've created, explore new horizons, and continue growing. By reflecting on your past, setting intentional goals, and embracing the unknown, you can shape a future filled with purpose and fulfilment.

Quote: "The best way to predict the future is to create it." – Peter Drucker

Summary: 1825 –
Think. Build. Thrive

The years between 18 and 25 are a canvas of infinite possibility—a time to dream, learn, and grow. This book has been your companion through this transformative period, offering insights, strategies, and stories to help you navigate the challenges and opportunities that define these formative years.

From mastering self-discipline and communication to embracing failure and leveraging the power of continuous learning, we've explored the tools and mindsets needed to build a life of meaning and purpose. Each chapter invited you to look inward and act outward, cultivating the habits, values, and skills that form the foundation of a fulfilling future.

Through inspiring case studies, actionable exercises, and moments of reflection, we've walked together towards a deeper understanding of what it means to thrive, not just in your twenties, but for a lifetime.

As you reach the final page, take a moment to look back— not just on the book, but on yourself. You are not the same person who started this journey. Every lesson you've absorbed, every question you've pondered, and every step you've taken have shaped the person you are today.

These years, so full of change and discovery, are just the beginning. The road doesn't end at 25, and the lessons don't stop here. You've planted seeds of growth and potential, and now it's time to nurture them.

The challenges you've faced and the triumphs you've celebrated have prepared you for what lies ahead. They've taught you to dream without fear, to fail without despair, and to grow without limits. The wisdom of these years is now yours to carry into the next chapter of your life.

A Call to Seek More

This book may end here, but your journey does not. The road ahead stretches endlessly, filled with opportunities to learn, create, and leave your mark. Carry with you the knowledge that the person you choose to become is shaped by the decisions you make every day.

1. Dream Boldly: Let your ambitions guide you towards goals that inspire and challenge you.
2. Act Purposefully: Align your actions with the values that matter most to you.
3. Seek Growth Relentlessly: Embrace every opportunity to learn, adapt, and improve.

You are the author of your own story, and the chapters ahead are unwritten. As you step into the next phase of your life, take the lessons of 1825 with you. Use them to create a life that is not only successful but meaningful, a life that reflects your highest aspirations and deepest values.

Final Thought:

"You are not defined by where you start, but by the road you choose to travel. The greatest stories are written by those who dare to walk their path. Let yours be one of courage, purpose, and endless discovery."

Remember These Four Things:

1. Do not think about what others will think about you. If you do think, then you have already lost the battle.
2. Do your best in what you do, and do not think about the result.
3. You do not need to push down on someone else to grow.
4. As long as you are alive, there are infinite possibilities, so do not give up.